CANDICE LIN

A HARD WHITE BODY

Contents

DIRECTORS' FOREWORD

This publication focuses on a series of exhibitions under the title **A Hard White Body** that have unfolded at Bétonsalon – Center for Art and Research & Villa Vassilieff, Paris; Portikus, Frankfurt am Main; and the Reva and David Logan Center for the Arts at the University of Chicago. In this evolving and multi-sited project, the artist Candice Lin weaves together reflections on the life and work of several historical figures—including novelist James Baldwin; herb woman and explorer Jeanne Baret, the first woman to circumnavigate the globe; and artist and naturalist Maria Sibylla Merian—articulating their stories in relation to the imperial history of porcelain and its scientific use in the nineteenth century. We are proud to present this thoughtfully researched and visually compelling project, which also engages with the histories of our institutions' respective cities, Paris, Frankfurt am Main, and Chicago, adding an element of specificity and urgency to each iteration.

Lotte Arndt and Lucas Morin curated **A Hard White Body/Un corps blanc exquis** at Bétonsalon – Center for Art and Research & Villa Vassilieff. At Portikus, **A Hard White Body, a Soft White Worm** was curated by Lotte Arndt, Lucas Morin, and Philippe Pirotte. At the Logan Center, **A Hard White Body, a Porous Slip** was curated by Yesomi Umolu. We acknowledge and thank the funders whose support helped us realize these exhibitions. At Bétonsalon – Center for Art and Research & Villa Vassilieff, funds were provided by the City of Paris, the French Ministry of Culture and Communication, the Île-de-France region, the Daniel and Nina Carasso Foundation, and Perspektive – Fund for Contemporary Art and Architecture. Portikus received generous financial support from the Hessische Kulturstiftung. The presentation at the Logan Center was made possible by the Andy Warhol Foundation for the Visual Arts, The Reva and David Logan Foundation, and friends of the Logan Center.

The exhibition at Bétonsalon – Center for Art and Research & Villa Vassilieff was realized in close collaboration with Hélène Maes, Curatorial Assistant; Rémi Amiot, Production Manager; and Audrey Pouliquen, Production Assistant. We also thank Mathilde Assier, Communications Officer, and Pierre Vialle, Administrator, who greatly contributed to the show, as well as Boris Atrux, Project Coordinator, and Virginie Bobin, Head of Programs at Villa Vassillieff, for her invaluable and generous guidance. Thanks are also due to Marie Sophie Beckmann, Goethe-Institut Fellow 2017; Lila Torquéo; and Samah Slim, who contributed to making the events program a success. We extend our thanks to Regina Barunke, Director of Temporary Gallery, Cologne, and Robert Leckie, Curator at Gasworks, London.

The exhibition at Portikus was realized in close collaboration with Christina Lehnert and Fabian Schöneich, Curators; and Claudia Famulok and Louisa Schmitt, Exhibition Coordinators; as well as Hendrike Nagel, Office Assistant. We extend special thanks to the installation team: Xenia Bond, Jakob Brugge, Jack Brennan, Franz Hempel, Hannah Fitz, and Matt Welch.

The exhibition at the Logan Center was realized in close collaboration with Katja Rivera, Assistant Curator; Alyssa Brubaker, Exhibitions Manager; Marcus Warren, Shop and Gallery Manager; and Peter Reese, Assistant Director of Logan Shops. We thank them for their expertise, patience, and good humor throughout the development of the exhibition and the installation process. We are grateful to the students at the University of Chicago who assisted with the installation: Sarah Okayli Masaryk and Jazmine Harris. Thanks for pre-installation assistance is also due to Ali Paydar, Timothy Van Ausdal and Chris Rusak. We also extend our thanks to the Logan Center Media Center team: David Wolf, Associate Director for Arts Technology; Ben Chandler, Assistant Director, Jonathan Logan Media Center; and Kent Lambert, Assistant Director, Hack

Arts Lab, who provided technical assistance for the show. And we acknowledge the Communications team: Ronia Holmes, Director of Communications, UChicago Arts & The Logan Center; Clare Austen-Smith, Digital Content Manager, UChicago Arts & the Logan Center; and Samantha Weiss-Hills, Assistant Director of Editorial Content, Logan Center. Special thanks are due to Christina Jensen, Former Associate Director of Development–Arts, and her team. For their guidance and help with the logistical details of this project, we thank Greg Redenius, Director of Facilities and Operations, and his team.

This publication provides a space in which to reflect on Lin's burgeoning practice, and we would like to thank the contributing scholars and writers, who have greatly expanded our thinking about her work: Lotte Arndt, Rizvana Bradley, Mel Y. Chen, Jih-Fei Cheng, and C. Riley Snorton. We are also grateful for the generous support for the publication provided by the Elizabeth Firestone Graham Foundation, Hessische Kulturstiftung, and François Ghebaly, Los Angeles.

We are indebted to the editors of this publication, Lotte Arndt and Yesomi Umolu, for their dedication to the artist and her work as well as for the care and attention that they brought to the publication. A Hard White Body benefited from the intelligence, precision, and skill of editor Amanda Glesmann. Studio ELLA created a thoughtful design, and we are grateful for the inventiveness and vision they brought to all aspects of the process.

Finally, we would like to express our deep and sincere gratitude to the artist, Candice Lin, for her steadfast dedication and tireless commitment to the production of the exhibitions and publication.

—Mélanie Bouteloup, Director, Bétonsalon–Center for Art and Research & Villa Vassilieff

—Bill Michel, Executive Director, the Reva and David Logan Center for the Arts at the University of Chicago

—Philippe Pirotte, Director, Portikus

EDITORS' FOREWORD

Working across sculpture, drawing, and video, Los Angeles–based artist Candice Lin unsettles intersecting power structures by developing speculative stories around historical and fictional characters. Lin activates the critical potential of organic materials, mobilizing contaminated objects, mold, and body fluids with the aim of disrupting racialized, gendered, sexualized, or ableist hierarchies and rendering porous the boundaries between discrepant bodies. This publication is produced in conjunction with a series of exhibitions at Bétonsalon – Center for Art and Research & Villa Vassilieff, Paris; Portikus, Frankfurt am Main; and the Reva and David Logan Center for the Arts at the University of Chicago that took as a starting point the material history of the "hard white body" of porcelain in imperial Western society. Across these exhibitions, known collectively as **A Hard White Body**, Lin created complex imaginative environments that brought material and non-human histories into conversation with the biographies of historical figures. In doing so, she thoughtfully and expertly revealed the ways that human and non-human agents are both embedded in and willfully contest hierarchical power structures and narratives.

The process of working with the artist on this project has been at once exploratory and collaborative. Lin's tireless curiosity and depth of inquiry is accompanied by a genuine desire to share her research and engage with her audiences. Her installations require time, attention, and care. For these exhibitions, through acts such as donating bodily fluids or monitoring the constantly changing states of the work, the staff at each venue became intimately implicated in Lin's production. In addition, as will be evident in this publication, central to Lin's practice is a desire to render her research material both present and accessible. She thereby invites viewers to think through with her the speculative histories that she presents.

These pages provide space in which to expand on the artistic and intellectual investigations framing **A Hard White Body** as well as Lin's broader practice. The book's design and structure reflect a constellation of inquiries and methodologies that guide the artist's work, from her rigorous research across the fields of history, material culture, science, and more to her dexterous handling of sculptural materials and her cross-pollination of knowledge and perspectives from artistic and scholarly worlds. The tactility of this publication, which demands attentive reading and handling, also draws influence from the artist's acute understanding of the materiality of objects and their capacity to enliven the senses—a feature that is apparent in her sculptural environments, which breathe, seep, ferment, and decay over time.

This volume includes a visual essay by the artist that interweaves text and image fragments to elucidate the multiple, contradictory, and complementary trajectories of her research. An essay by writer and curator Lotte Arndt provides a reading of the complex and constantly evolving strata of histories that underpin **A Hard White Body** and charts the evolving forms the project took across the exhibition venues. Further, an interdisciplinary cohort of distinguished scholars have contributed their reflections. Rizvana Bradley, Assistant Professor of Film and Media Studies and African-American Studies, Yale University, provides a comprehensive discussion of Lin's work and argues for the importance of critical fabulation and speculative historical activation to the artist's practice. An essay by Mel Y. Chen, Associate Professor of Gender and Women's Studies, University of California, Berkeley, and Jih-Fei Cheng, Assistant Professor of Feminist, Gender, and Sexuality Studies, Scripps College, explores the status of scientific knowledge, its connection to the humanities, and its relationship to contemporary perspectives on the environment, gender, class, and race. Finally, a dialogue between the artist and C. Riley Snorton, Professor of English Language and Literature and Gender and Sexuality Studies, University of Chicago, elucidates the ways in which material histories intersect with human and non-human bodies and considers the imbricated histories of race, gender, and scientific thought.

Together, the publication's design and the diverse perspectives offered within speak to the transdisciplinary approaches that constitute the artist's multivalent projects. Creating a lasting document of Lin's burgeoning practice, this volume presents A Hard White Body as a compelling example of the ways in which an artistic practice can produce new forms of inquiry.

—Lotte Arndt, Co-curator of A Hard White Body/Un corps blanc exquis and A Hard White Body, a Soft White Worm

—Yesomi Umolu, Curator of A Hard White Body, a Porous Slip

ELECTIVE AFFINITIES

LOTTE ARNDT

"Is it possible to construct a story from 'the locus of impossible speech' or resurrect lives from the ruins?"—Saidiya Hartman[1]

"In the ruins left by the modern dream, we need to relearn to make history with the others, through the others, at the others' risk."—Isabelle Stengers[2]

Candice Lin's A Hard White Body entangles the stories of people, plants, and other matter from across centuries and continents. In this meticulously researched project Lin cultivates the hidden complicities and symbiotic relations across a large variety of mediums, ever mindful of their potential mutual endangerment. The work was presented in a series of exhibitions across Europe and the United States between 2017 and 2018 in entropically changing forms that articulated the historical charge of Lin's materials, weaving their contexts together in critical fabulations wherein precarious bodies struggle in the ruins of global capitalism and its imperial foundations.[3] Following her materials' entangled transnational journeys, Lin engages what I would like to call "elective affinities,"[4] referring to Leela Gandhi's discussion of "affective gestures that refuse alignment along the secure axes of filiation to seek expression outside, if not against, possessive communities of belonging."[5] She contests the racial and sexual classifications introduced by positivist sciences and colonial power, searching for unspoken "intimacies" across taxonomic divides.[6] Rather than focusing on individual identities, Lin's work operates through assemblages that can be understood to function as drag, drawing on what Renate Lorenz terms the "productive connections of natural and artificial, animate and inanimate, to clothes, radios, hair, legs, all that which tends more to produce connections to others and other things than to represent them."[7]

1. . . . . Saidiya Hartman, "Venus in Two Acts," Small Axe 26 (June 2008): 3.

2. . . . . Isabelle Stengers, "Préface," in Le champignon de la fin du monde. Sur la possiblilité de vivre dans les ruines du capitalisme, by Anna Lowenhaupt Tsing (Paris: La découverte, 2017), 13. Translation by the author.

3. . . . . Having been involved in the project as a curator, my reading follows the structure of the three exhibitions loosely. It jumps in time, crisscrossing the assemblages presented at each venue and seeking to bring the works into conversation with writers and ideas that we have been discussing over the past two years, including ideas developed during the public program Disturbing Objects, Disquiet Objects: Going Beyond Classificatory Certainties in Paris and Cologne. For more information, see http://www.betonsalon.net/spip.php?article736.

4. . . . . My use of the term "elective afinities" draws on postcolonial theorist Leela Gandhi (see note 5) and the discussions around chosen families in non-normative theory and practice, and responds critically to Johann Wolfgang von Goethe's (1749–1832) eponymous novel.

5. . . . . Leela Gandhi, Affective Communities. Anticolonial Thought, Fin-de-Siècle Radicalism, and the Politics of Friendship (Durham, NC: Duke University Press, 2006), 10.

6. . . . . Lisa Lowe, The Intimacies of Four Continents (Durham, NC: Duke University Press, 2015), 35.

7. . . . . Renate Lorenz, Queer Art: A Freak Theory (Bielefeld: Transkript, 2012), 21.

SOFTNESS AND THE POROSITY OF THE HARD WHITE BODY

For the exhibition *A Hard White Body/Un corps blanc exquis*, organized by Bétonsalon – Center for Art and Research, Paris, Lin sculpted a fragile room entirely from unfired porcelain and kept it moist with a distilled liquid composed of urine, water from the Seine river, and medicinal plants. Surrounded by thin plastic sheets that fluttered with every peripheral movement, the room comprised a bed, a suitcase, a violin, and clothes that spilled all over the place. The floor was wet, and the whole space stank. Cracks ran through the sculpted walls, which had been perfectly white the day of the opening. After some weeks, green and orange mold grew, insects crawled out of the fissures, and liquid residues stagnated in the small puddles between the porcelain sheets. The sculpture's instability and flux increased daily (pp. 35–39, 45–46). One morning, after the plastic sheeting that protected it overnight was removed, mushrooms sprouted. In another instance, a visitor stepping into the porcelain room left big footprints in the soft clay. I describe the installation in great detail because its entropic material evolution raises a conceptual question: how does this malleable, moist body, itself a multitude of promiscuous, heterogeneous, mingling matter, challenge the idea of porcelain as a "hard white body"?

One aspect of Lin's installation centered around James Baldwin's novel *Giovanni's Room*, a gay love story from 1956 that takes place in a cramped space that is oppressive in its poverty and narrowness and yet provided a refuge for a socially unacceptable desire that is often linked with internalized self-loathing. Beyond this literary reference, Lin's creation of a porcelain room activated a complex colonial history that was interrogated in the research material presented in the exhibition. Developed in China, porcelain's recipe had remained a secret in Europe until its ingredients were discovered and it began to be produced in Meissen, Germany, in 1710. In a 1712 letter to his colleague Father Louis-François Orry, the French Jesuit priest François Xavier d'Entrecolles described porcelain as "an exquisite white body."[8] He detailed his

8. . . . . Letter from Père d'Entrecolles to Père Orry (1712) in *Lettres édifiantes et curieuses concernant l'Asie, l'Afrique et l'Amérique*, vol. 3, ed. M. L. Aimé-Martin (Paris, Société du Panthéon Littéraire, 1843), 208, 211.

longing to attain knowledge of its production, a desire that led him to acts comparable to today's industrial espionage. The racially anxious language of his description is keen to preserve the whiteness and impermeability of this highly prized ceramic body and celebrates its resistance to cracking or discoloration. Porcelain was widely admired for producing perfectly white vessels that allowed for the consumption of colonial products like tea and coffee without risk of staining.

As a stain-resistant surface, porcelain can be read as a metaphor for a fantasy of self-sufficiency grounded in racial superiority. Lin focuses on the contradictions in this ideology. As we learn, the precious material proves to be impermeable only at first sight. When the French scientists Louis Pasteur and Charles Chamberland used porcelain in the nineteenth century as a filter for bacteria, they realized that its fine pores allowed for smaller organisms to pass; this discovery was highly important in establishing the field of virology.[9] Pasteur and Chamberland's filters were used at the 1893 World's Columbian Exposition in Chicago, a celebration of the four-hundredth anniversary of Christopher Columbus's arrival in the "New World" in 1492, which welcomed twenty-seven million visitors. This world's fair aimed to highlight technological progress, the nation state, and the imperial narrative of Columbus's conquest. Through its exhibits and architectural layout it contrasted ethnographic displays of indigenous and non-Western societies with demonstrations of technological advancement, its gleaming neoclassical buildings projecting a pinnacle of cultural attainment underscored by its popular moniker "The White City."

FEMALE STOWAWAYS AND METAMORPHOSING COCOONS

At Portikus, Frankfurt am Main, Lin's exhibition *A Hard White Body, a Soft White Worm* brought together fragments of the now-fired and broken porcelain room; an abortifacient peacock flower; James Baldwin; Jeanne Baret and Maria Sybilla Merian—two female imperial travelers distinct in terms of class and education; and several

9 . . . . . See Bert Hansen, "The Filter of Life," *Distillations* 2, no. 3 (2015): 6–7, and Bruno Latour, *The Pasteurization of France*, trans. A. Sheridan and J. Law (Cambridge, MA: Harvard University Press, 1988).

hundred hungry silkworms.

Born in Frankfurt in 1647, Merian grew up surrounded by renowned engravers and printmakers (including her stepgrandfather Theodore de Bry, who made some of the first images of the "New World" to be publicly disseminated in Europe). She may have been the only European woman who voyaged exclusively in pursuit of her art and science in the seventeenth and eighteenth centuries.[10] In her fifties she traveled for two years to Suriname to pursue research on metamorphosis. In 1707 she published her book *Metamorphosis Insectorum Surinamensium* (Transformation of Surinamese Insects), which weaves together drawings, scientific considerations, and travel accounts.[11] Merian was one of the few Europeans to credit the African and indigenous slaves and workers on whose labor she relied.[12] Still, as an imperial traveler who witnessed the atrocities perpetrated at the Surinamese sugar plantations, she was ostensibly complicit in the colonial exploitation and slavery that pervaded the Dutch colony (fig. 1).

The installation at Portikus included a painted plastic sheet titled *Under the Shadow of the Peacock Flower* that formed a translucent ceiling. Through its milky transparency the grayish contours of a peacock flower and a silkworm, drawn by Lin from Merian's engravings, were visible (p. 77). Lin based these drawings on the brown vestige of the image visible on the backside of a print—a blurred silhouette created by "the acidic burn of the pigments reacting to the paper over two centuries of time."[13] Formally, the dark contours of the ceiling painting resonated with the painted windows at Bétonsalon – Center for Art and Research. Titled *We Demand the Right for Opacity*, it referred to Martinican philosopher Édouard Glissant's advocacy for opacity as a means of resisting imperial power and its relentless quest for control through knowledge and classification.[14]

In moments of silence a gentle crunching was audible in the exhibition space. It was the sound of hundreds of

10 . . . . . For further discussion of Merian's travels, see Londa Schiebinger, *Plants and Empire, Colonial Bioprospecting in the Atlantic World* (Cambridge, MA: Harvard University Press, 2004), 30.
11 . . . . . Ibid., 109.
12 . . . . . Ibid., 11.
13 . . . . . See Candice Lin, "Licking the Wound: Three Works from Pacific Standard Time: LA/LA," *X-tra* 20, no. 4 (Summer 2018), accessed online, https://x-traonline.org/article/licking-the-wound-three-works-from-pacific-standard-time-la-la/.
14 . . . . . Édouard Glissant, *Poetics of Relation*, trans. Betsy Wing (Ann Arbor, MI: The University of Michigan Press, 1997), 189–94.

Fig. 1
Left: Verso of Maria Sibylla Merian's engraving of Caesalpinia pulcherrima (Peacock flower plant) in Metamorphosis insectorum Surinamensium (The Metamorphosis of the Insects of Surinam), 1705. RB 633752, The Huntington Library, San Marino, California

Right: Verso of "The execution of breaking on the rack," in John Stedman's Narrative of a Five Years' Expedition Against the Revolted Negroes of Surinam, 1796. Smithsonian Libraries, Washington, D.C.

These images were originally included as research materials in the exhibition A Hard White Body, a Soft White Worm, Portikus, Frankfurt am Main

silkworms eating dried mulberry leaves as they progressively covered the fragments of the porcelain room with their excrement, their skin, and their dead bodies. While their soft forms and close-to-transparent color stood in sharp contrast to the uneven, hard surfaces of the white porcelain blocks and bricks, the silkworms were bound to the space by their historical ties with transnational trade routes and the accordant intimacies between people and things from afar (p. 84). Silk had been a lucrative international commodity in China for at least five thousand years. By the eighteenth and nineteenth centuries silk production was of major economic importance in many European countries, and Merian—who had relatives engaged in the silk trade in Frankfurt—searched for an alternative to the silkworm in Suriname. In the nineteenth century a silkworm disease in the French countryside considerably diminished local farmers' incomes, and it was widely suspected that this blight had foreign origins. Pasteur ultimately determined that it had been inflicted by a local microbe.[15] His research on filters and vaccines introduced a language of purification, isolation, and tidiness that finds striking parallels in the vocabularies of nationalism, ethnic cleansing, and racial purity.

FILTER SYSTEMS, RACIAL PURIFICATION, AND TEMPORAL DRAG

In the exhibition *A Hard White Body, a Porous Slip* at the Reva and David Logan Center for the Arts at the University of Chicago, Lin pursues her work on filters and liquids by pointing to the resonances between the mania surrounding contamination and purification evident in hygienic discourses from the end of the nineteenth century. In the years preceding the World's Columbian Exposition, Chicago was gripped by a typhoid epidemic that threatened the success of the event's proclamation of technological progress and cultural advancement. When the typhoid bacillus was identified in 1880, examining water supplies for bacteria became the new standard, but this practice had not yet been established in Chicago.[16] In this context the fair's organizers relied on

15 . . . . . See Latour, *The Pasteurization of France*.

16 . . . . . Bronwyn Rae, "Water, Typhoid Rates, and the Columbian Exposition in Chicago," *Public Health Review* 2, no. 2 (2015), accessed online, http://www.publichealth.northwestern.edu/nphr/2015-v2i2/3-rae.html.

the Pasteur-Chamberland filter to provide clean drinking water for visitors. Water was a core element of the fair, as its architectural centerpiece was a large pool that represented the imperial ocean voyage of Columbus. Resonating with this monument while also inversing its doctrines, the pool of porcelain casting slip that Lin installed at the Logan Center contained cloudy water, and though filtration devices were present, they seemed to fail at purification (p. 105). Here, a dirty, earthy, burnt fecal scent meandered through the rooms, raising suspicions about unhygienic conditions.

At the Logan Center, Lin introduced yet another filter by using bone-charcoal pigment to paint a mural on the walls (p. 117). Her activation of this material recalls the violent working conditions of the plantation system and their material sedimentation: bone charcoal is made from livestock bones. Photocopies and research material displayed alongside the distillation system in the center of this room suggested a connection to the experiences of the Chinese coolie laborers documented in the 1873 report directed by Imperial Commissioner Chin Lan-Pin, which was initiated by the Imperial Chinese court to assess working conditions on Cuban plantations. One worker wrote: "We are old and weak and It Is only uncertain whether we shall die in a depot or in a fresh place of service, or cast out as useless by the roadside; but it is certain that for us there will be neither coffin nor grave, and that our bodies will be tossed into a pit, to be burnt with those of horses and oxen and to be afterwards used to refine sugar."[17]

As this commentary suggests, bone charcoal is emblematic of a plantation model that is founded on the disposability and interchangeability of people, plants, and animals and the destruction of a system of interdependent cohabitation in favor of an economy of scale.[18] Still, it is precisely in these desolate conditions that intimate encounters take place across imperial division lines and humans, plants, and other beings from the extremities of the global trade routes meet, clash, and coalesce. On the plantation, bone charcoal was used for refining and purifying sugar, turning its color from brown to white. Sensitive

17 . . . . . See *The Cuba Commission Report: A Hidden History of the Chinese in Cuba* [1876] (Baltimore: The Johns Hopkins University Press, 1993), 110.

18 . . . . . See Tsing, *Le champignon de la fin du monde*, 39.

19 . . . . . For further discussion of this aspect of Lin's practice, see the text by Mel Y. Chen and Jih-Fei Cheng on pages 92–102 of this volume.

to the metaphorics inherent to this process,[19] Lin emphasizes the parallels between porcelain and bone charcoal. As filtration materials, both are loaded with racialized imagery and entangled colonial histories.

Throughout the three exhibitions visitors were reminded of their own bodily presences. At Bétonsalon – Center for Art and Research they had to kneel down to see and read the documents, drawings, books, and sculptures on the brick installation *The Wake*. They had to navigate the sun's changing position and walk around to find the right angle from which to watch *The Beloved*, the video that was screened on the plastic sheeting. And they were called to contribute their urine to a distillation circuit where it was combined with herbs and water to produce a liquid that would keep the installation moist (fig. 2). Notably, the urine was collected in a porcelain urinal, a gesture that turned the paradigmatic Duchampian readymade back into a useful basic commodity and thus questioned the supposed neutrality of the exhibition space and its purported distance from a realm of bodily hygiene and intimacy structured by gender, race, and sexuality.

In providing stand-to-pee devices made of porcelain that allowed visitors with vaginas to use the urinal, a form originally designed for cis-male use, Lin's work humorously disrupted binary gender conceptions and male-centered art histories. Countering the policing of public toilets as spaces in the urban geography of anonymous sexual encounters—a terrain that has been devastated by the securitarian individualism, biopolitical control of promiscuity, and protectionism introduced in the frame of the AIDS epidemic[20]—Lin installed the urinal in a highly visible position at the exhibition's entrance, thus turning notions of private and public upside down. This element of the installation can also be read as a wink at the omission of Elsa von Freytag-Loringhoven, the Dada artist who submitted a porcelain urinal signed R. Mutt for a collective exhibition before Marcel Duchamp "famously" solidified this conceptual gesture under the title *Fountain*.[21]

Just as von Freytag-Loringhoven's work has been widely left out of art historical accounts, Lin's exhibition

20 . . . . . See Elisabeth Lebovici, *Ce que le SIDA m'a fait* (Zurich and Paris: JRP Ringier and La maison rouge, 2017).

21 . . . . . Julian Spalding and Glyn Thompson, "Did Marcel Duchamp steal Elsa's urinal?" *The Art Newspaper*, November 2014, http://ec2-79-125-124-178.eu-west-1.compute.amazonaws.com/articles/Did-Marcel-Duchamp-steal-Elsas-urinal/36155.

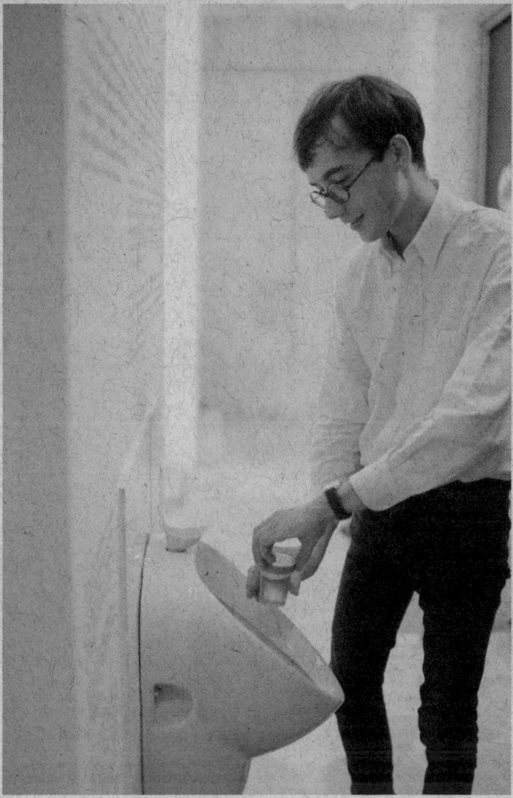

Fig. 2
Donation of urine during A Hard White Body/Un corps blanc exquis, Bétonsalon – Center for Art and Research, Paris, September 2017

follows the journey of a peculiar imperial traveler whose remarkable trajectory is poorly recognized: Jeanne Baret, a French herb woman from the Loire Valley who left her peasant life by means of a borrowed identity. She cross-dressed as a man in order to embark aboard the French ship *L'Étoile* on the famous voyage navigated by Louis-Antoine de Bougainville in 1766. As with the other figures she refers to in her exhibition, Lin relates to Baret's journey as a gesture of transhistorical solidarity, striving to connect the herb woman's life to present-day feminist and queer struggles. Elizabeth Freeman characterizes this voluntary anachronistic bonding as "temporal drag," a tactic that allows for identifications with gender-norm subverting practices across time.[22] Temporal drag can thus relate to embodiments of past struggles against normative and essentializing conceptions of sexuality without supposing that historical and contemporary conditions correspond directly with each other. Lin's drawing of Baret depicts her dressed as a man and bearded, radicalizing her "freaky" features[23] and affiliating her story with the many invisible narratives of suffering endured by those struggling to escape persecution for their race, gender, or sexuality.[24]

SLIPPERY GROUND, LIQUID CONNECTIONS, AND TOXIC EMBODIMENTS

Throughout the exhibition's stages, Lin worked with liquidity as the state in which bodies lose their fixed delimitations. She elaborates: "I think of liquid as caretaking, as moisturizing, as keeping something supple and tender, able to bend. Liquid that keeps something fed, growing like a plant, or in a state of wet potential: unfixed, unfired, un-certitude."[25] The exhibition at Bétonsalon – Center for Art and Research was kept moist with a dripping sprinkler system and the caring gestures of the staff. At Portikus, the room was poorly lit in blue, murky light, evoking an underwater feeling that was underscored by the ingestion

22 . . . . . Elizabeth Freeman, "Packing History; Count(er)ing Generations," *New Literary History: A Journal of Theory and Interpretation* 31 (2000): 728–29.

23 . . . . . In using the term "freak" I follow Renate Lorenz, who explains that it "has been used to collect the most diverse ways of taking on or producing a certain distance to dominant norms or to the normalizing practices of white, heterosexual, masculine or feminine US-Americans or Europeans without this difference in turn producing a unified and recognizable category. I would like to refer to such performance as 'radical drag.'" See Lorenz, *Queer Art*, 166.

24 . . . . . See the dialogue between Candice Lin and C. Riley Snorton on pages 48–58 of this volume.

25 . . . . . See Candice Lin, "J.B.," *BS* 22 (2017): 13, accessed online, http://betonsalon.net/IMG/pdf/bs22-final-complet.pdf.

of a hot detox tea mixed with distilled urine that welcomed visitors in the cold German winter months. Finally, at the Logan Center the installation was submerged in a pool full of porcelain casting slip mixed with increasing volumes of distilled piss. The fired porcelain fragments, bricks, images, and books were placed in the pool like elements of an archipelagic landscape; depending on their porosity or impermeability they curled, lost their color, bloated, or molded. Both materially and linguistically, the exhibition opened to a polysemic field, evoking in the glutinous slip of the wet clay both the slipping of viruses through the porous porcelain filter and the uncontrolled, accidental slips of the tongue that voice repressed anxieties and unconscious desires.

Liquids operate as vehicles for entanglement, constituting and bending bodies among each other: the distilled urine used in the installations, for instance, carried the hormones and toxins ingested by and contained in the bodies that excreted it. They were inhaled or swallowed by visitors in the form of the installation's mist and humidity, or in the hot tea, and thus connected seemingly discrete bodies. Thinking about reciprocity in relation to interdependent bodies implies conceiving of promiscuity "at the other's risk,"[26] even to the point of a potentially mortal endangerment, a position that stands in radical opposition to an ideal of safety based on individual protection and (collective) isolationism. Conversely, the detox tea served at Portikus evoked the idea of a healthy, natural body cleansed of damaging influences such as endocrine disruptors or detrimental working conditions. Notably, all human and non-human components of Lin's installation are interdependent, connected by their shared environment, by language, and by their symbiotic relationships with fellow beings. Lin shows, for example, a drawing of tobacco leaves that resemble faces and thus allude to the racialized description of leaves infected by the Tobacco Mosaic Virus as having gone "mulatto"(fig. 3).[27] While here illness is presented through racialized language, Lin relates to the leaves by subjectifying them, allowing for identification across divisions between species. She investigates the intimate relationship between toxic

26 . . . . . Stengers, "Préface," 13.
27 . . . . . See Jih-Fei Cheng, "'El tabaco se ha mulato': Globalizing Race, Viruses, and Scientific Observation in the Late Nineteenth Century," *Catalyst. Feminism, Theory, Technoscience* 1, no. 1 (2015): 1–41.

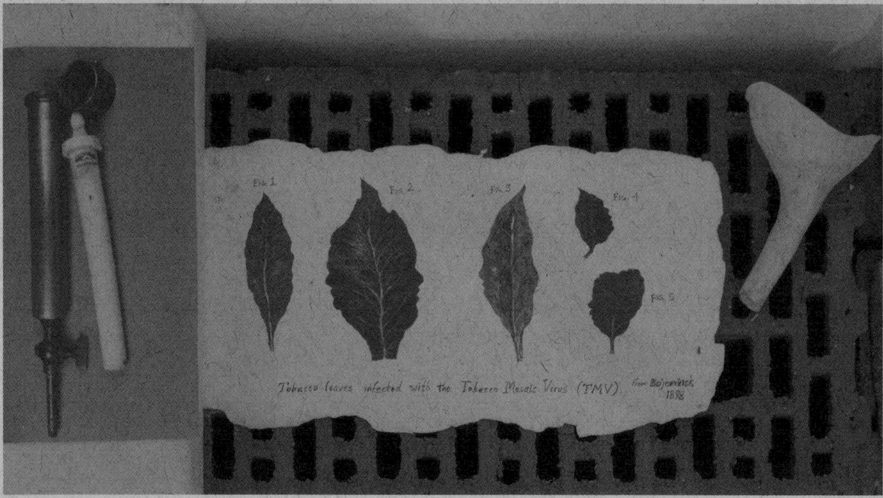

Fig. 3
Drawing of tobacco leaves infected with Tobacco Mosaic Virus. The edges of the leaves resemble human profiles. Installation view of **A Hard White Body, a Soft White Worm**, Portikus, Frankfurt am Main, 2018

environments and notions of race, sexuality, and class. For the artist, borrowing from queer theory and the work of writers Mel Y. Chen, Vanessa Agard-Jones, and Jih-Fei Cheng, toxicity is a potential source of pleasures and radical decentering, even as its destructive effects impact bodies unequally.[28]

In Baldwin's writing, water is repeatedly presented as a metaphor for fundamental transformation, an irresistible attraction, and a menace. Crossing the Atlantic Ocean allowed him to spend years far enough from the United States to be able to focus on his craft in a social context in which he was less involved. In *Giovanni's Room* he describes a space that feels like it is "underwater" and associates this with a suffocating feeling.[29] But he also tells us that the protagonist, David, underwent a "sea change" in this room, and discusses in a draft autobiographical sketch the significance of his use of the metaphor of the sea, which attracts him to the point that he will risk losing himself in the water, never to return from a swim.[30]

Lin weaves this personal dimension of Baldwin's relationship with the sea together with an interrogation of the conditions that enable affective communities to arise. In his essay "Take Me to The Water" Baldwin interrogates the sense of transversal solidarity in his European exile. A black American in Paris, he describes the absence of Algerians upon his return to the French capital in 1961, and the rumors of their torture, detainment, and murder.[31] And he wonders if anybody in the city would look for him if he were to disappear without leaving a trace, as was the case when he was imprisoned for several days.[32] Highly engaged in the civil rights movement in the United States even as his fellow activists derided him for his homosexuality,[33] he critically interrogates his relative disconnection from the anti-colonial struggles surrounding him in France. The exhibitions included a drawing by Lin based on a famous photo of graffiti on St. Michel Bridge that denounces the bloody repression by the French state of a peaceful

28 . . . . . See Lotte Arndt and Lucas Morin, "A Hard White Body," BS 22 (2017): 4–6, accessed online, http://betonsalon.net/IMG/pdf/bs22-final-complet.pdf.

29 . . . . . See James Baldwin, *Giovanni's Room* (1956; repr. London: Penguin Books, 2007), 67–76.

30 . . . . . James Baldwin Papers, SC MG 936, Box 1, Folder 4, Schomburg Center for Research in Black Culture, New York Public Library.

31 . . . . . James Baldwin, "Take Me to the Water," in *Collected Essays* (1955; repr. New York: Penguin Books, 1998), 374–75.

32 . . . . . Baldwin, "Equal in Paris," in *Collected Essays*, 101–16.

33 . . . . . See Eldridge Cleaver, *Soul on Ice* (1968; repr. New York: Dell Publishing / Random House, 1991), 128–129.

Algerian demonstration for independence in Paris held on October, 17, 1961.[34] Only decades later, a plaque was installed at the bridge, commemorating the drowning of numerous Algerians in the Seine river. Thinking about the river as a bearer of history, Lin filled the sprinkler system that moistened the sculpture at Bétonsalon – Center for Art and Research with Seine water, thus charging the porous sculptural body with the memory of anti-colonial struggles.

Lin likewise refers to the Atlantic Ocean as a repository for histories of violence, drawing from Christina Sharpe's book *In the Wake: On Blackness and Being* and its discussion of the Africans who despairingly jumped from slave ships or were thrown overboard by crews seeking to conserve water, lighten the load, or claim insurance. Lin's use of liquids animates Sharpe's concept of "residence time," the time that organic matter takes to disappear from the environment. Sharpe explains that "atoms of those people who were thrown overboard are out there in the ocean even today. They were eaten, organisms processed them, and those organisms were in turn eaten and processed, and the cycle continues."[35] Lin's reference to Sharpe's and Baldwin's records of the sea as an opaque bearer of memory counters the use of water in the symbolic staging of Columbus's conquest that was at the core of the 1893 exposition and its quest for pure drinking water for Chicago (pp. 114–15). Narration once again unfolds through the matter, entropy, and cross-contamination residing in the liquidity of the pool, in which objects are infused and lose their shape, their hardness, and their distinctiveness, transitioning to as yet unknown states.

RUINS, SURVIVAL, AND STORYTELLING

Liquidity, porosity, fragmentation, and organic composure contrasted materially at all three venues with the language of hardness and purity around porcelain and race. Losing the softness of its Parisian form, the broken remnants of the porcelain room were shown at Portikus and the Logan Center in their fired state. They were assembled in a scene of destruction, a landscape of porcelain chunks, dispersed bricks, cracked elements of drapery, nearly unrecognizable pieces of clothing, and

34 . . . . . Here I am referring to the exhibition work Candice Lin, *Ici on noie les algériens* (Here They Drown Algerians), graphite on paper, 2017.

35 . . . . . Christina Sharpe, *In the Wake: On Blackness and Being* (Durham, NC: Duke University Press, 2016), 40–41.

discarded books, evoking a tenuous life gathered together in pieces that do not compose a whole (p. 111).

At Portikus, construction elements could still be identified: bricks, plastic sheets, and small electric lightbulbs recalled the paragraphs of Baldwin's novel describing the constant work undertaken by Giovanni to embellish the room and create a "home" for the lovers. At the Logan Center, these attempts were revealed to be a hopeless enterprise. The porcelain pieces arranged in the water recalled the burned vestiges of the World's Columbian Exposition—in January 1894 a fire broke out that in little more than three hours ravaged the proud edifices of the so-called White City. (The buildings were made of a mixture of painted white plaster, cement, and jute fiber, which was highly flammable.) Visitors to Lin's exhibition had the sense of having arrived just after the catastrophe. Their bodies were oriented toward harsh, resisting matter immersed in stagnant liquids. A racial reading imposes itself: transposing material qualities to the field of affect, Sara Ahmed proposes to understand "hardness [...] not [as] the absence of emotion, but a different emotional orientation towards others. The hard white body is shaped by its reactions: the rage against others surfaces as a body that stands apart or keeps its distance from others."[36] While the soft skin of the wet porcelain evoked a sense of porosity and tenderness, the hardness of the fired remains reveal the divisions fabricated by imperial history and the plantation system.

Ahmed's reflections resonate with the historical references in Lin's three wall paintings in bone-black pigment. One showed the burned buildings and wreckage of the 1893 Chicago Columbian Exposition—the ruins of imperial history. Another depicted the burning sugar fields of the Haitian revolution; in absence of historical images, visualizing this revolt relied on descriptions. Lin's video *The Beloved* references C. L. R. James's description of the uprising, which led to the first black republic in history: "From Le Cap the whole horizon was a wall of fire. From this wall continually rose thick black volumes of smoke, through which came tongues of flame leaping to the very sky. For nearly three days the people of Le Cap

36 . . . . . Sara Ahmed, *The Cultural Politics of Emotion* (Edinburgh: Edinburgh University Press, 2004), 5.

could barely distinguish day from night, while a rain of burning cane straw, driven before the wind like flakes of snow, flew over the city and the shipping in the harbor, threatening both with destruction."[37] The third painting diagrammed the process of sugar refining using bone charcoal. As a pure technical mode of representation, the memory of people's lives lost in this process disappears from the scene, recalling that modes of narration can erase or inscribe vulnerable presences and demand transtemporal care and kinship. In the middle of the room a pit-fired ceramic skull dispensed a customized scent of burned buildings, burned sugarcane, burned bones, sewage, and a tincture of poisonous plants (pp. 114–16).[38] This mixture's olfactory nuances wove together allusions to the ferocious exploitation of colonized, enslaved people and indentured laborers with testaments to anticolonial resistance and the ruins of modernity's proud ambitions.

Lin's work evokes the destructive effects of imperial violence and its aftermath and searches for material and narrative modes of countering them. Scattered in pieces, the fragmented sculpture called for interrogation of the way stories are recomposed in incomplete arrangements. This is not a passive contemplation of a desolate landscape but an approach to ruins that demands the displacement of attention to what could be considered insignificant, striving to identify adequate modes of narration through careful attention to these troublesome assemblages.[39]

None of the figures in these moving environments remained fixed. An ambiguous relation to displacement and anti-homes is the condition of all of the human and non-human inhabitants of Lin's assemblages, with their fragile matter and multiple times and places. They navigate the divisions of the imperial inhospitalities with which they find themselves misaligned and in constant reorientation. It is in this sense that the soft skins and scattered fragments of Lin's porcelain installations allow precarious affinities to become visible in glimpses, associating silkworms and plants; poison and remedies; muddy liquids and organic filters; imperial ruins, racial

37 . . . . . C. L. R. James, *The Black Jacobins: Toussaint L'Ouverture and the San Domingo Revolution* (1938; repr. London: Penguin, 2001), 70–71.

38 . . . . . This custom scent was created by the artist with assistance from Timothy Van Ausdel and Chris Rusak from The Institute for Art and Olfaction, Los Angeles.

39 . . . . . See also Stengers, "Préface," 8.

metaphors, and queer linguistics. Through elective bonding, her complex sculptural and narrative articulations give rise to fragile genealogies and transtemporal drag that may yet point to inhabitable, feral futures.

BÉTONSALON – CENTER FOR ART AND RESEARCH

PAGES 31–46
INSTALLATION VIEWS OF
A HARD WHITE BODY/
UN CORPS BLANC EXQUIS

SEPTEMBER 6–DECEMBER 23, 2017

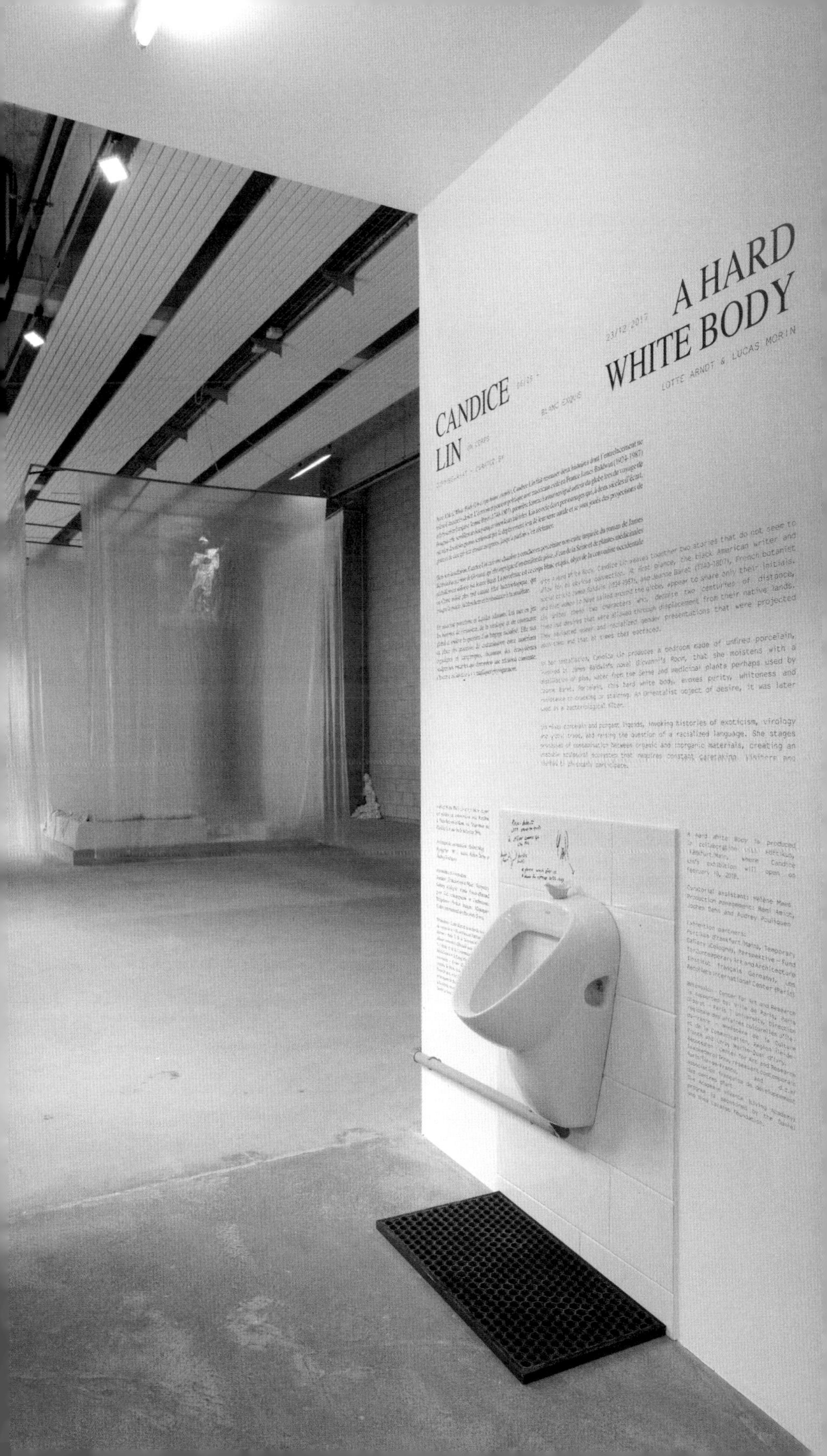
CANDICE
LIN
23/12/2017
A HARD
WHITE BODY
LOTTE ARNDT & LUCAS MORIN

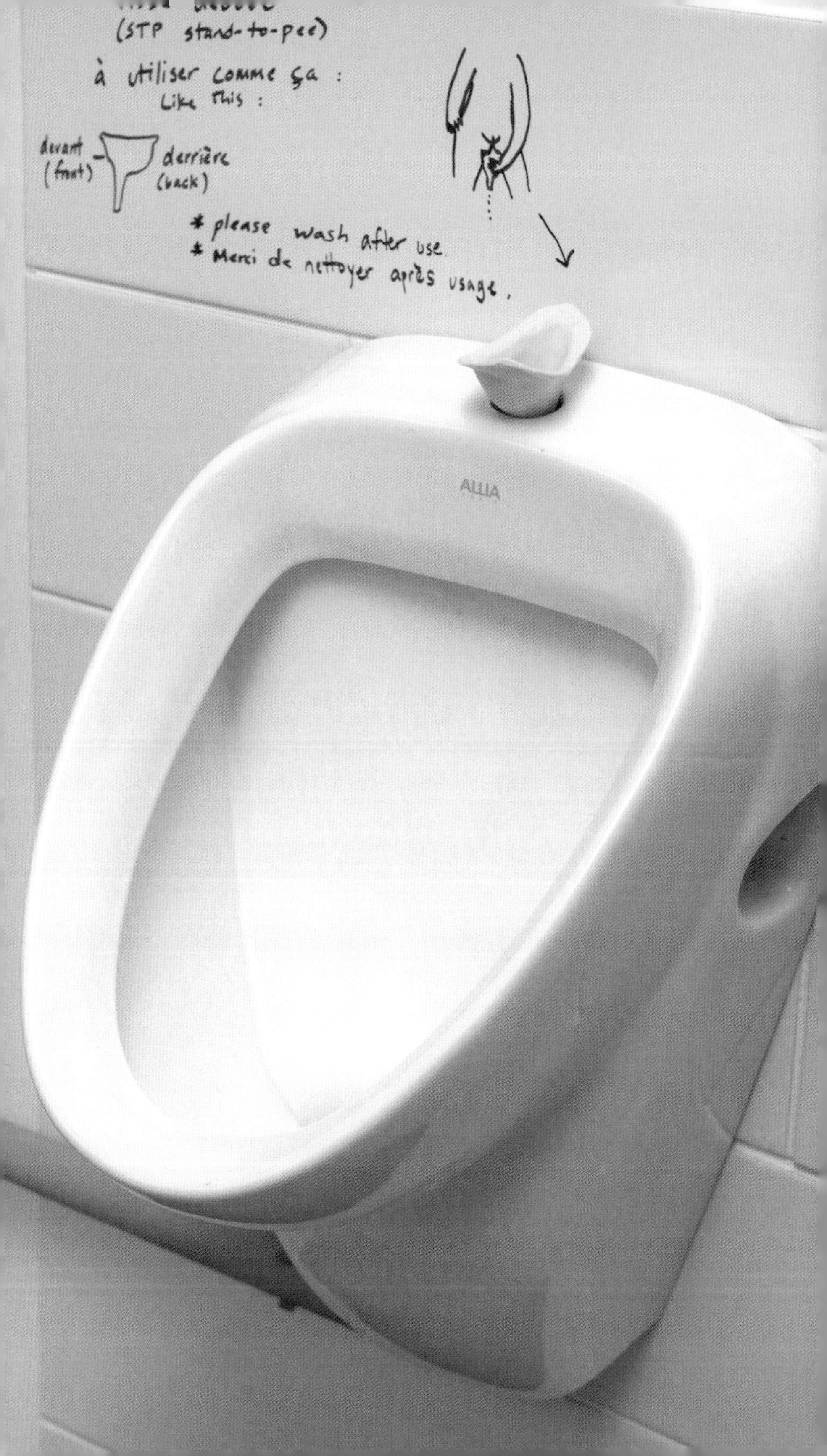
(STP stand-to-pee)
à utiliser comme ça :
Like this :
devant
(front)
derrière
(back)
* please wash after use.
* Merci de nettoyer après usage.
ALLIA

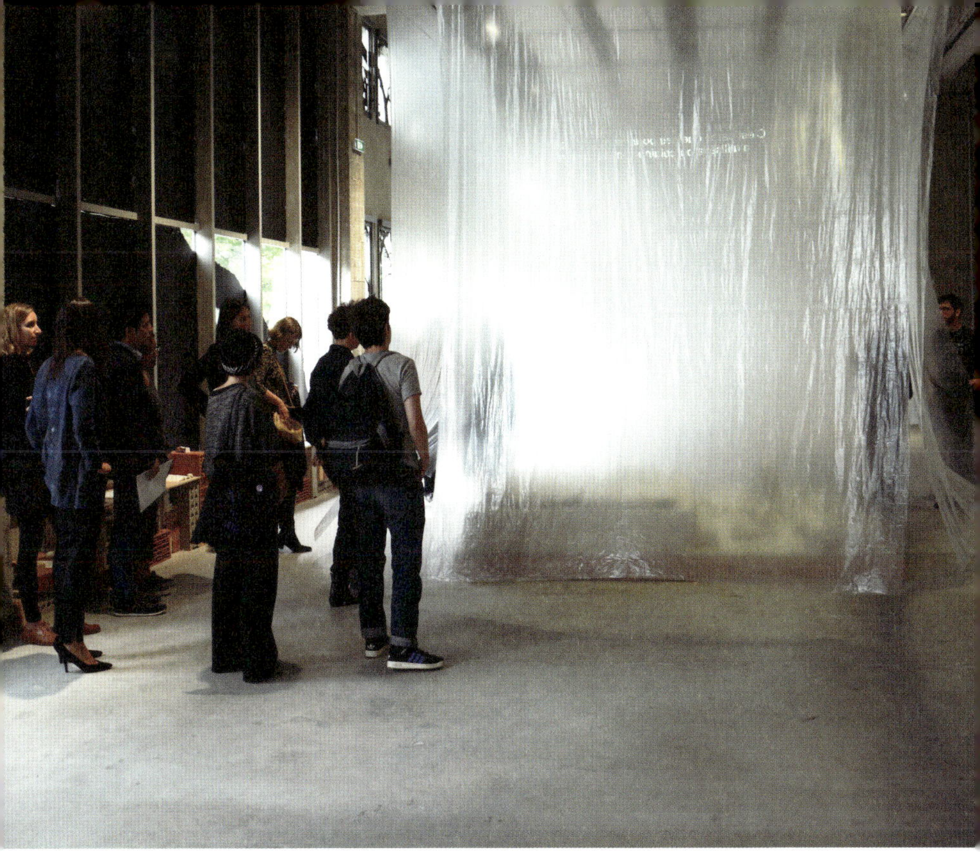

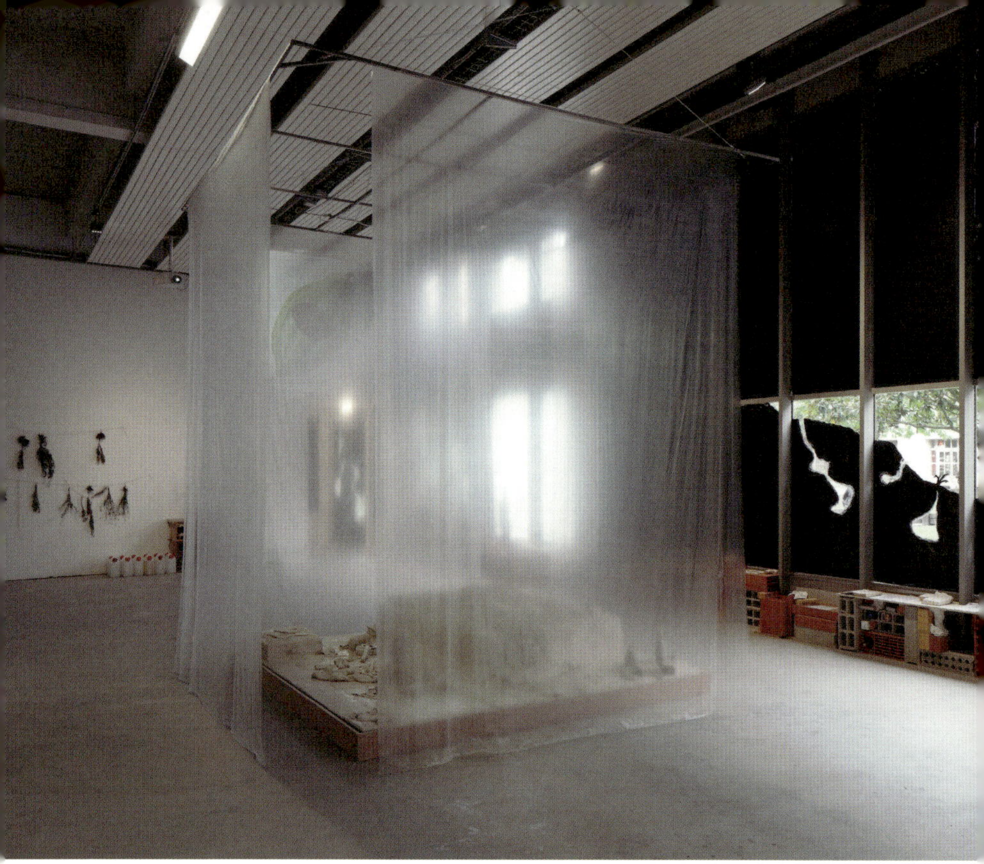

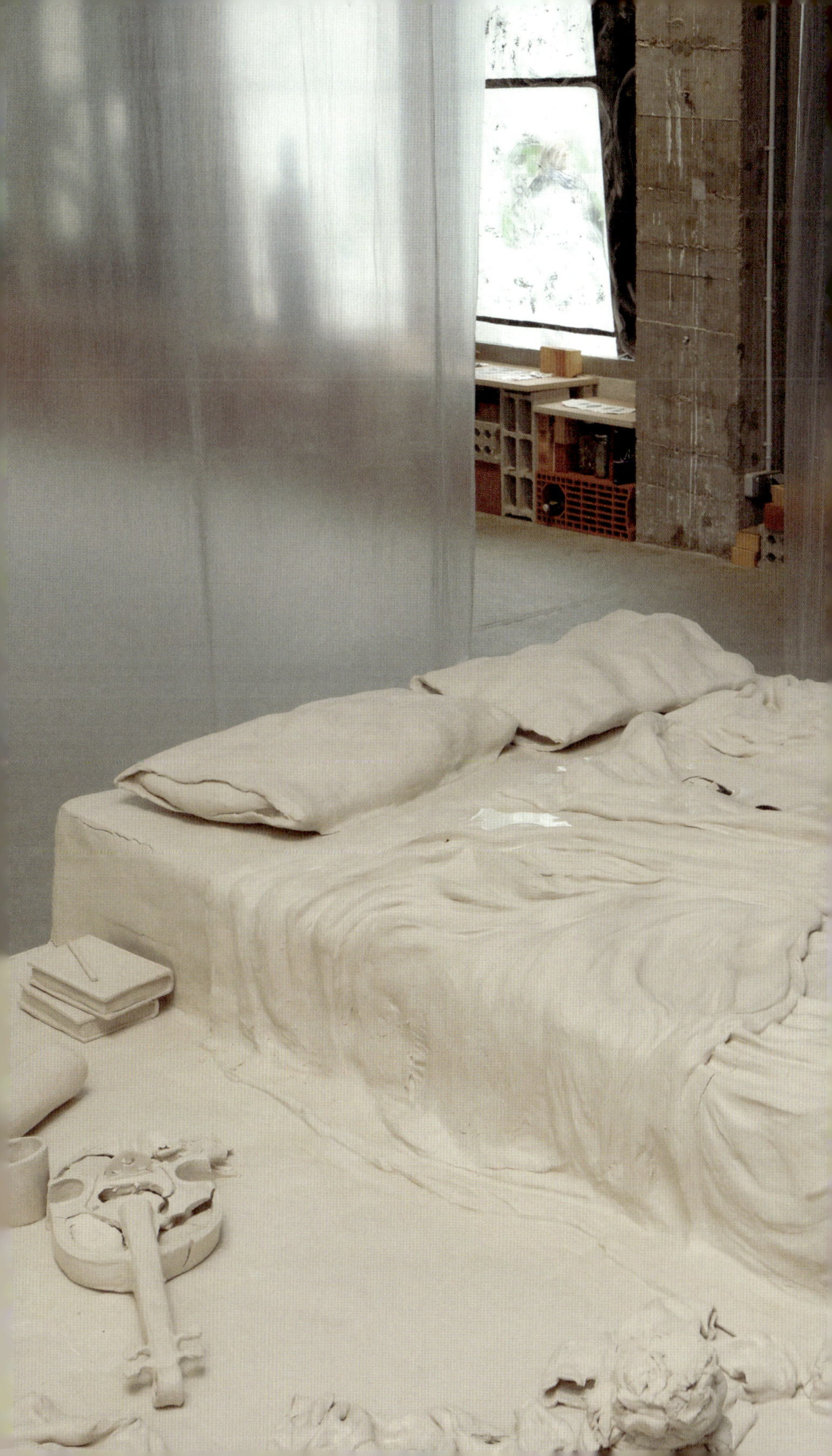

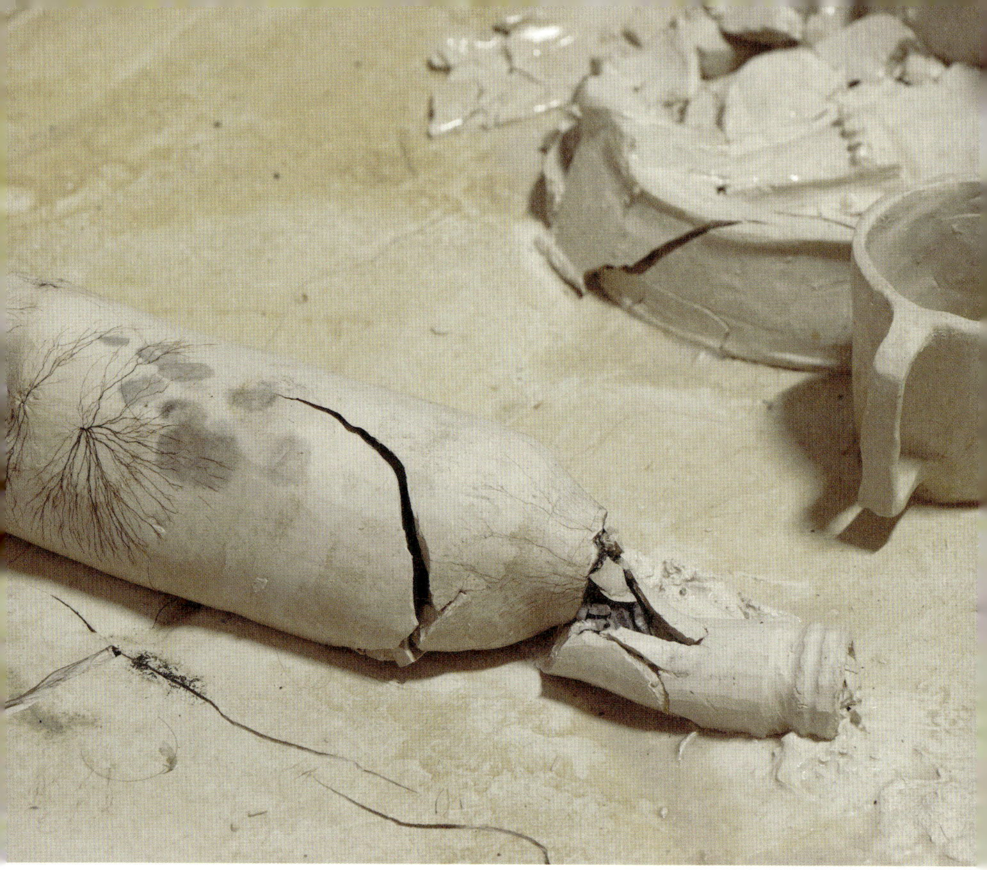

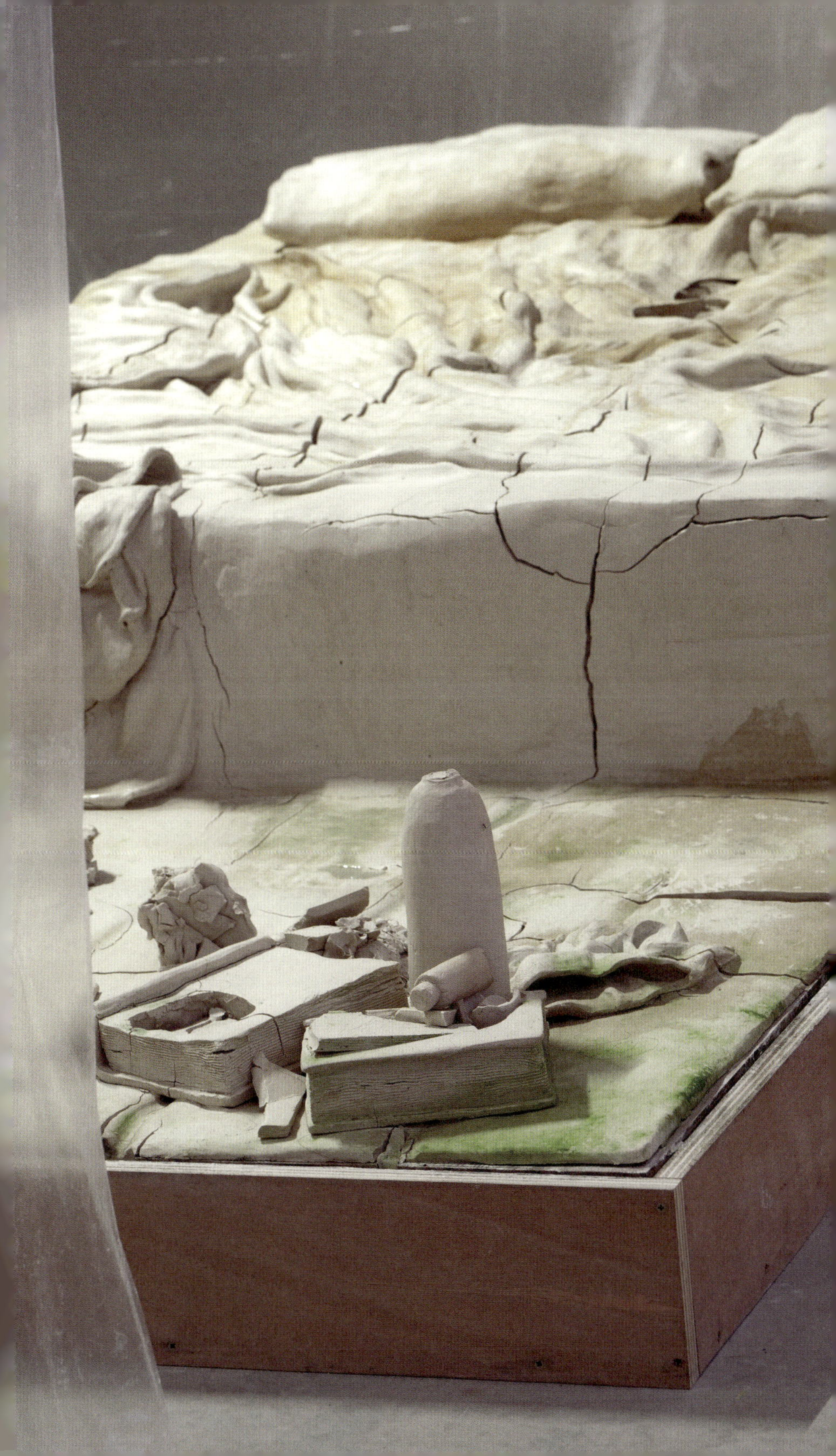

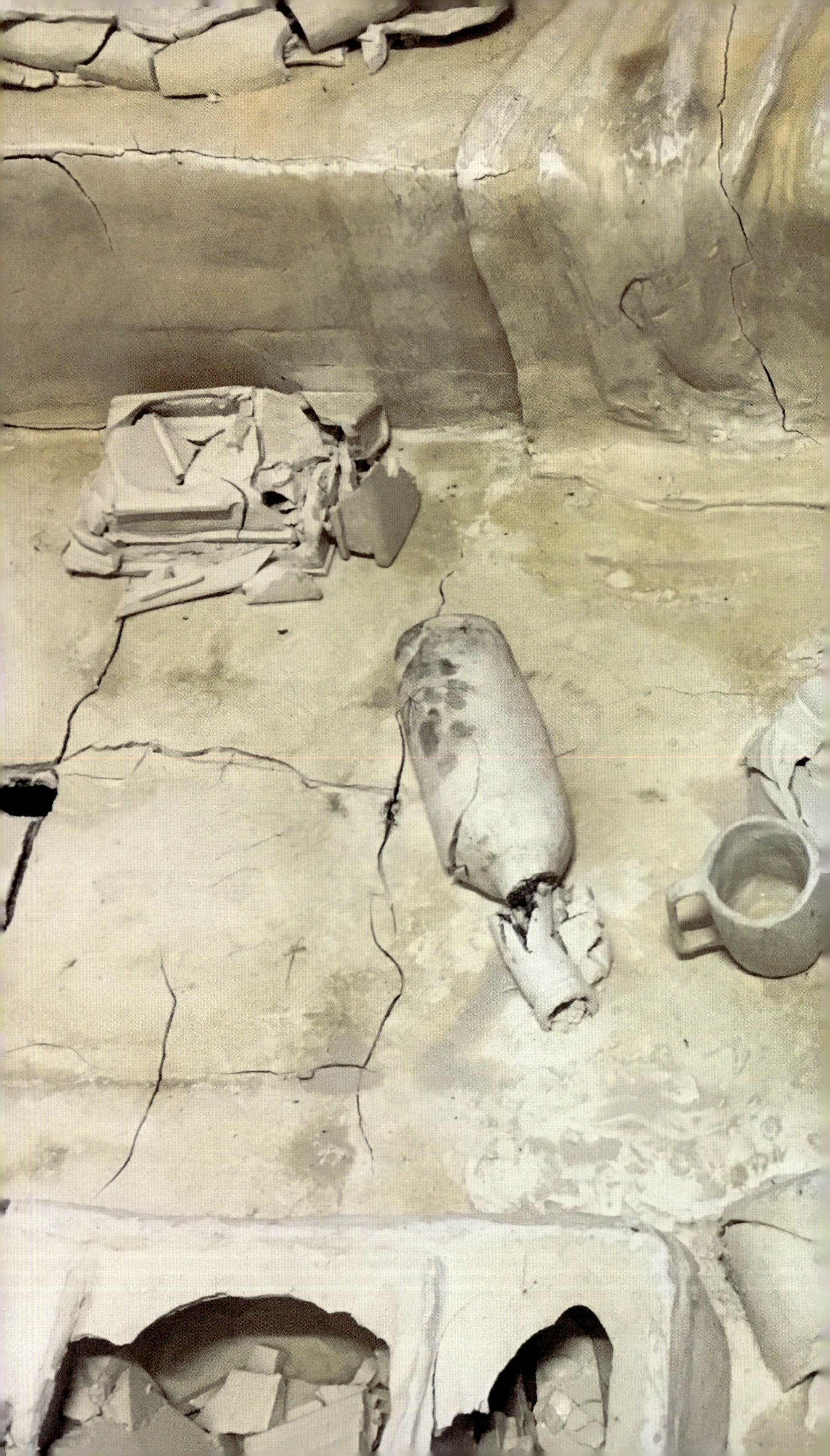

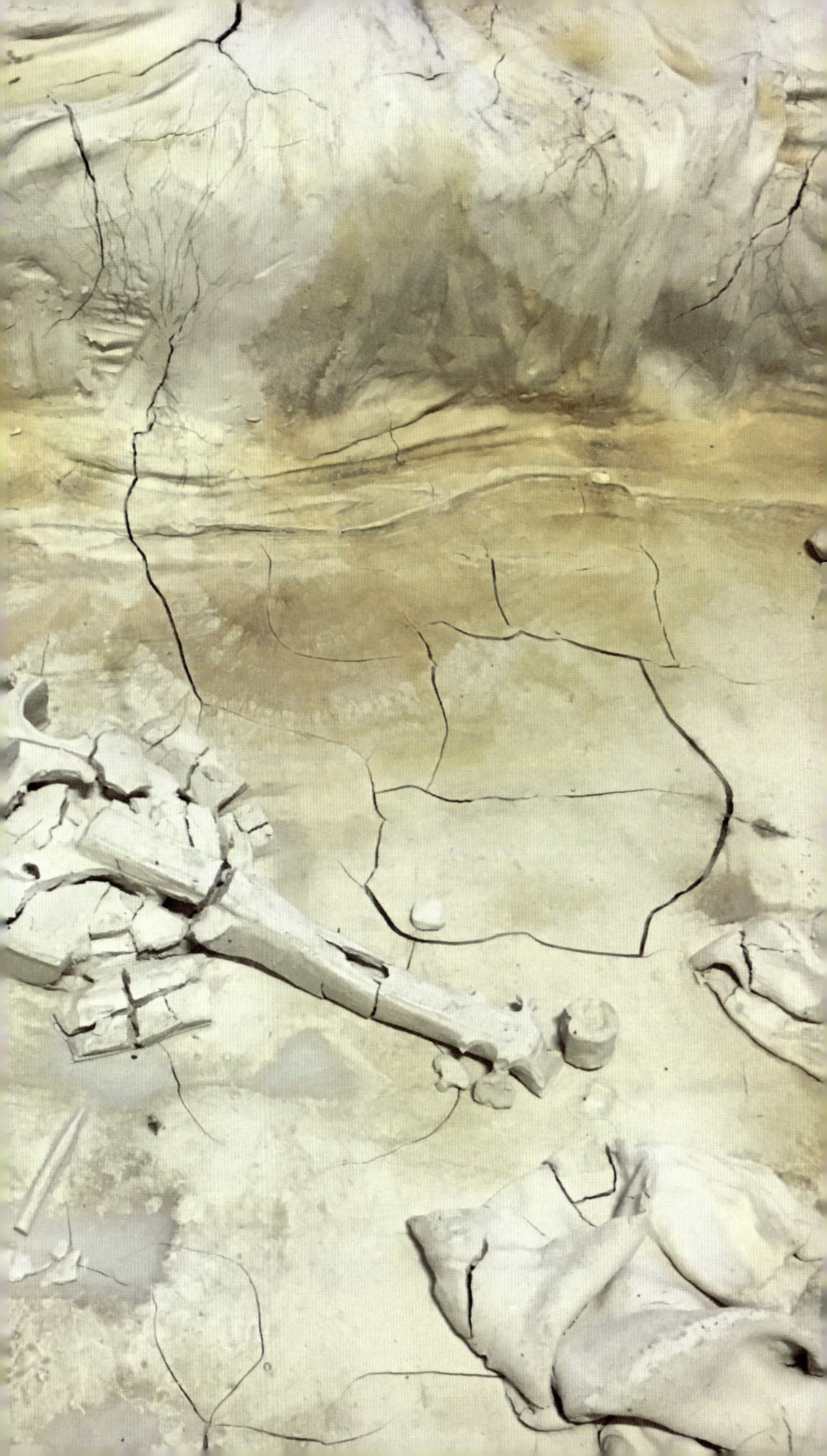

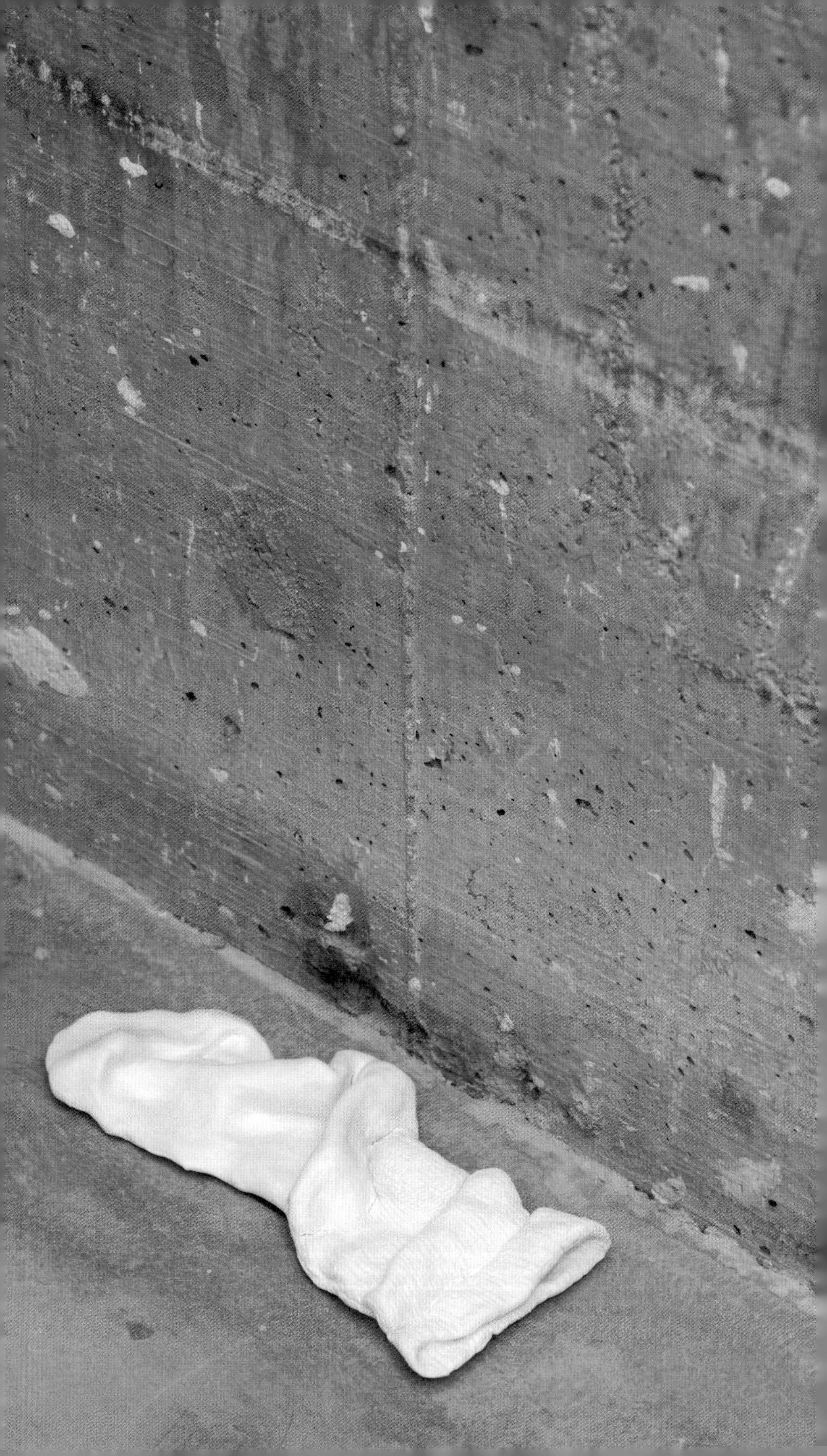

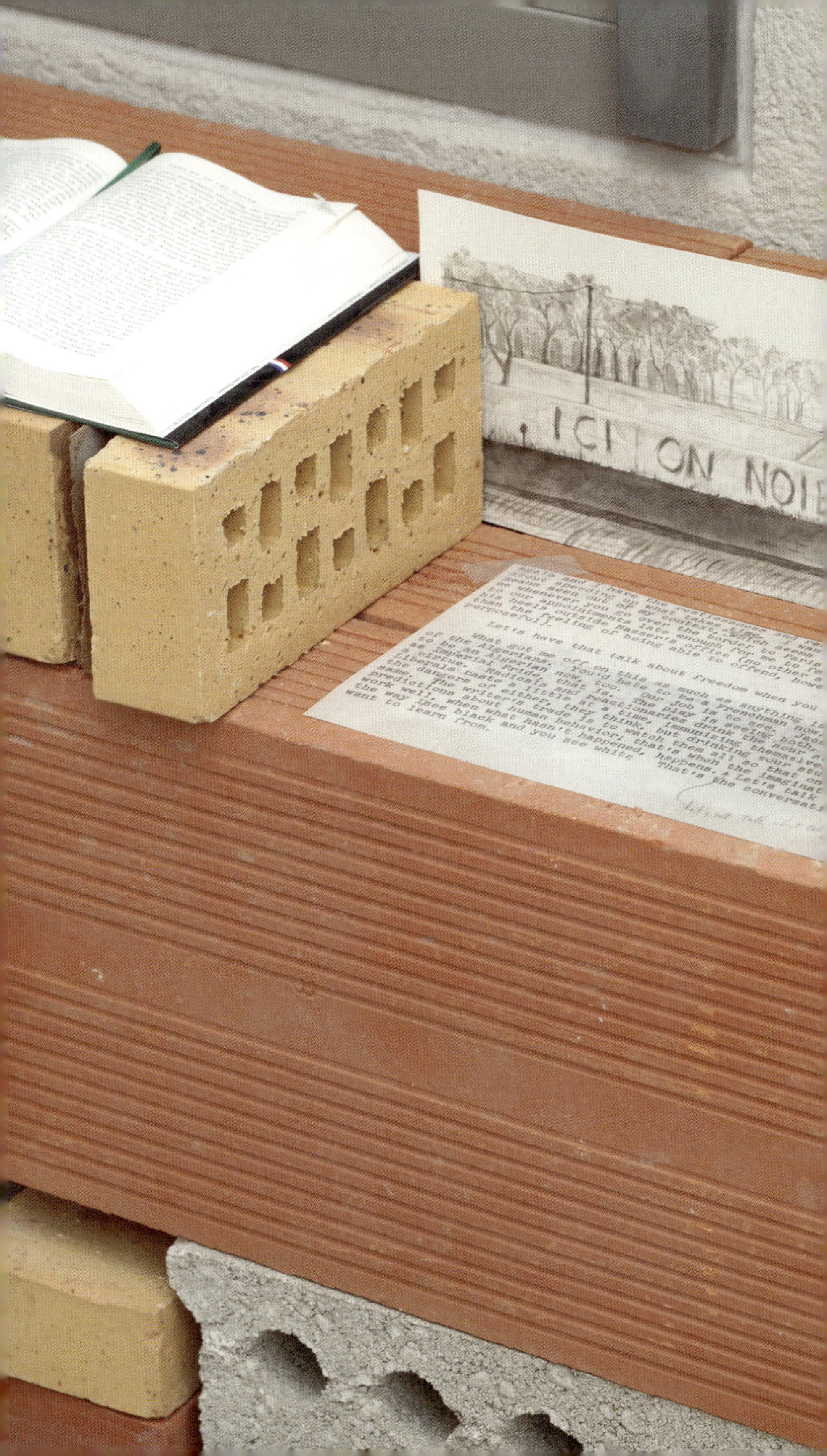
ICI ON NOIE

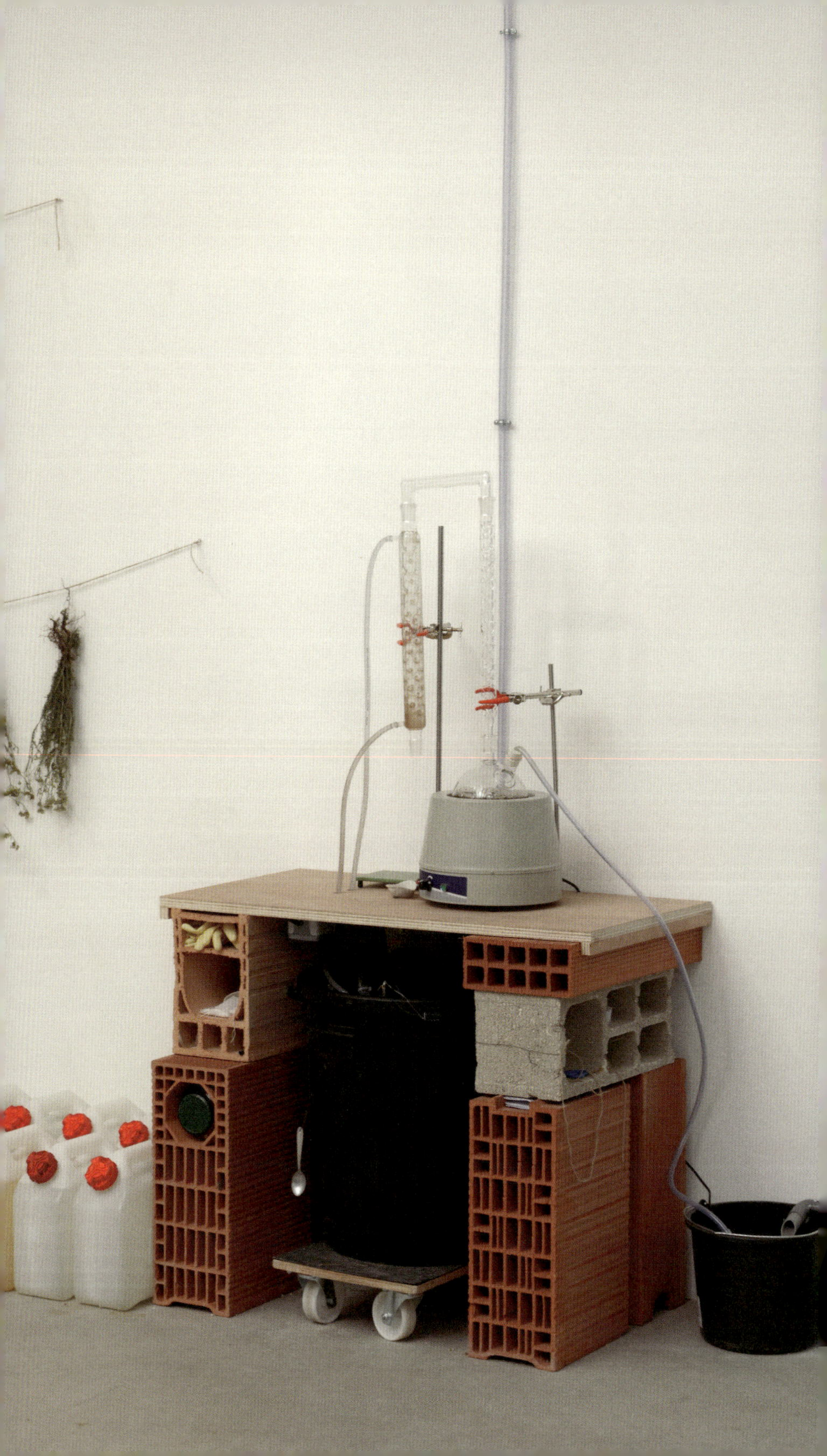

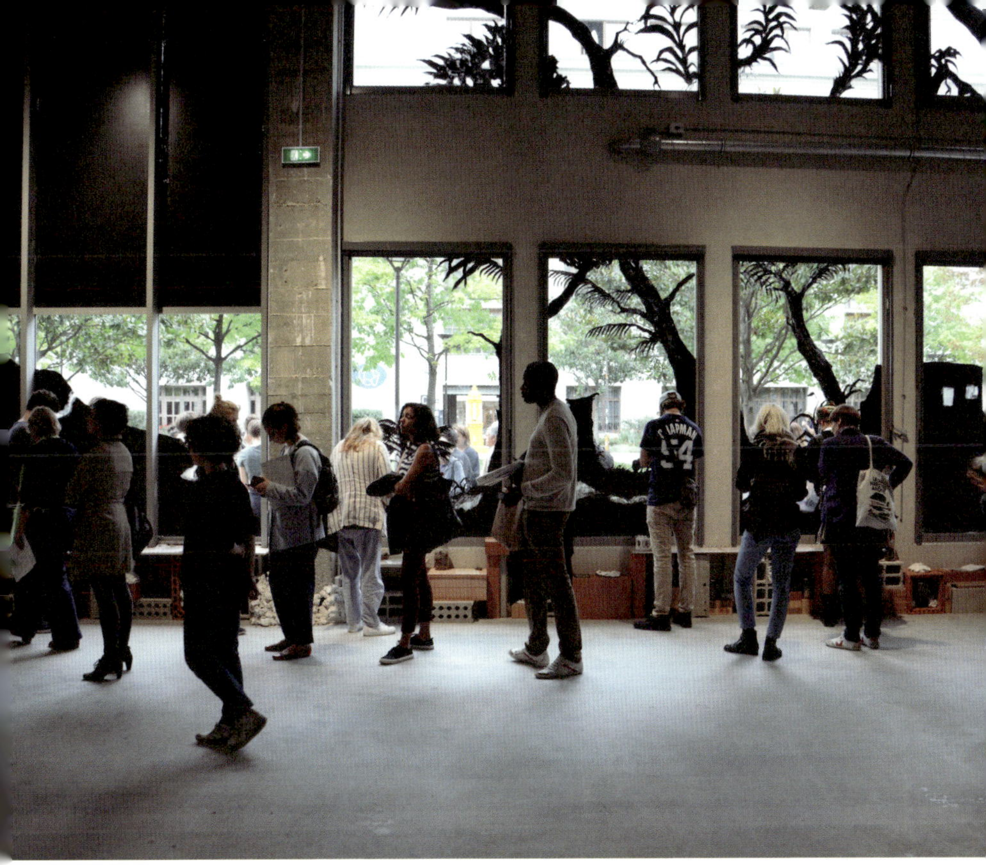

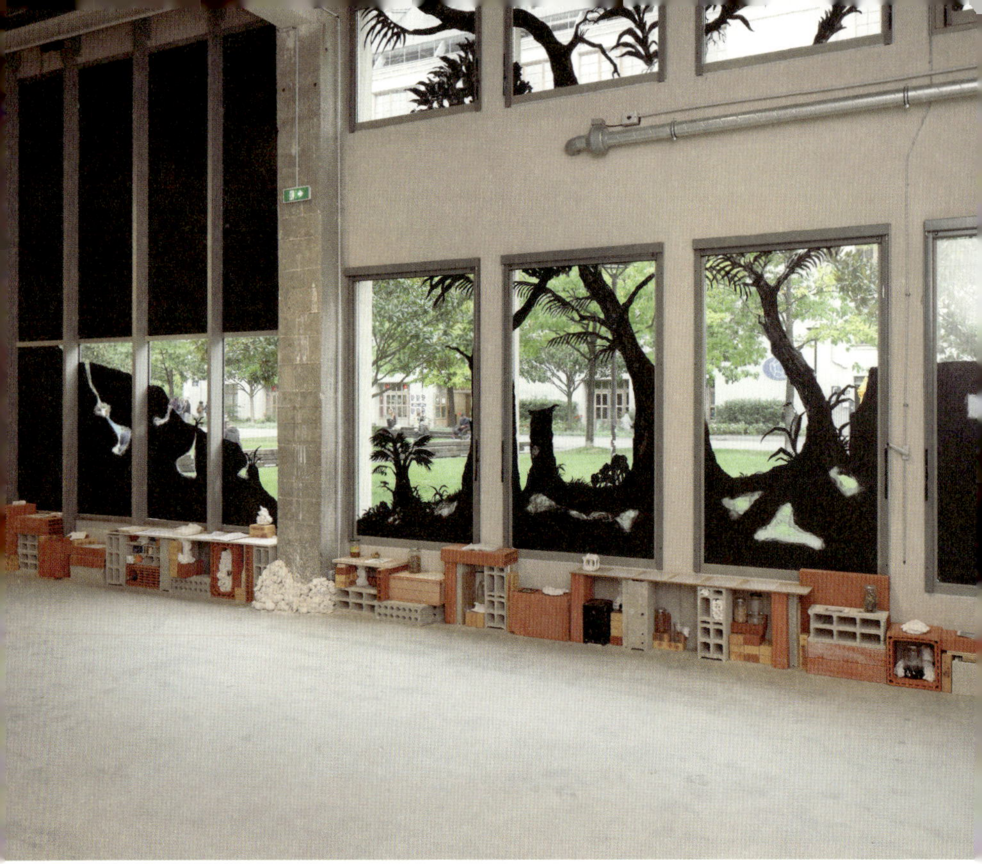

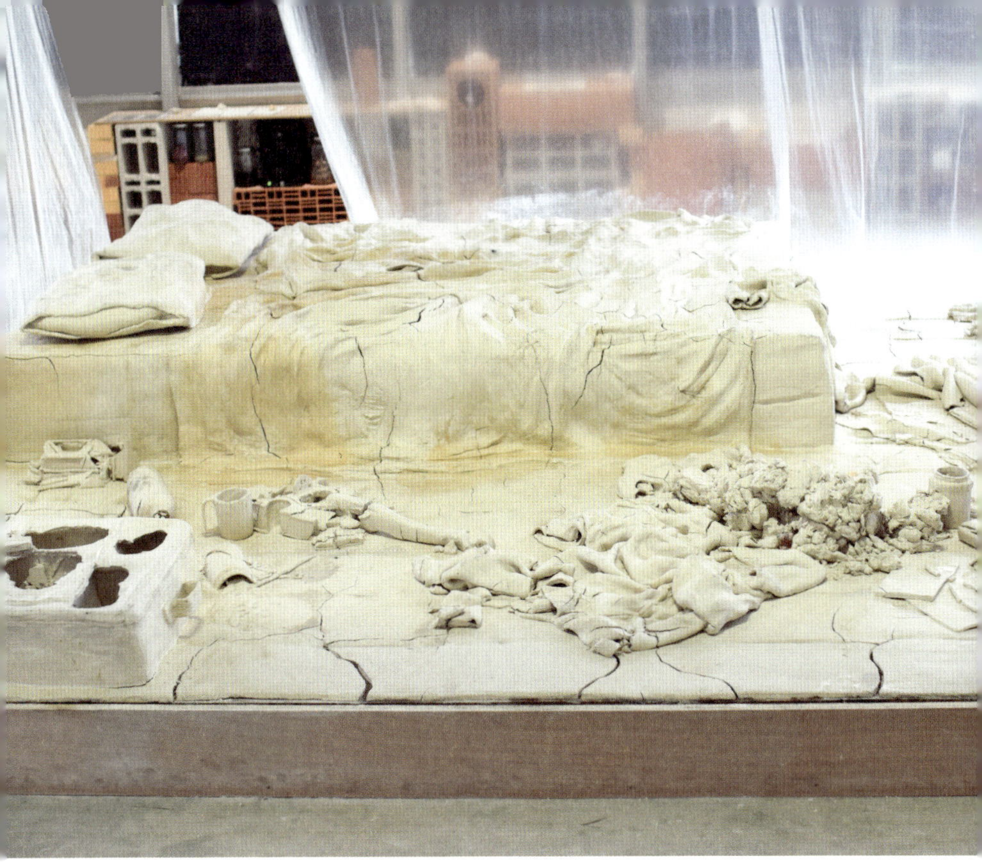

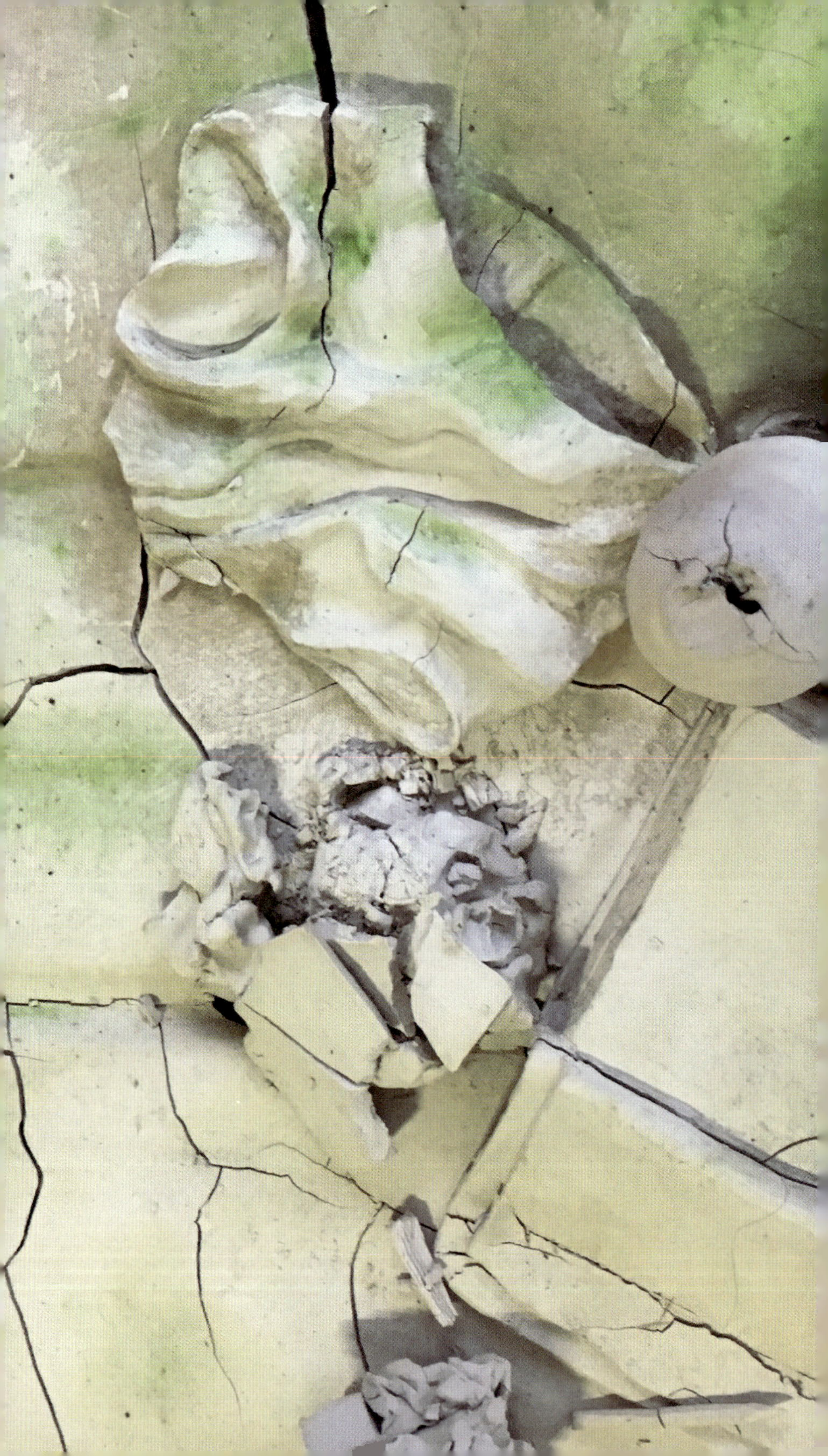

IN DIALOGUE

CANDICE LIN AND C. RILEY SNORTON

CANDICE LIN: When we first met, I heard you give a lecture about the gendering of race that addressed the beginnings of the field of gynecology through the use of enslaved black women and examined the aspects of racial and gendered "passing" at work in Ellen and William Craft's fugitive slave narrative. I was excited about the overlaps your lecture had with what I was currently researching for my exhibition *A Hard White Body* at Bétonsalon – Center for Art and Research, Paris, in 2017 that looked at the history of porcelain in relationship to specific human histories and sought to tease out imbricated relations of race, gender, and sexuality, as well as to think about displacements in geography and time. There was something about the way you use material histories (of sheets, surgical instruments, glass) in your writing that I related to.

The way you described the Crafts' story made me rethink the question of anachronism. I had been wrestling with the historical narrative of Jeanne Baret, who was perhaps the first woman to circumnavigate the globe and did so by cross-dressing as the male valet to her lover and employer Philibert Commerson. A doctor on board their ship attested that Baret's ability to gender-pass was attributable to her broad shoulders, strong physical ability, and sun-browned and roughened skin. The other people I was working with on the exhibition read this not as racialization but rather as an issue of class, and I was trying to understand how to think through this episode from the eighteenth century, when race was still being formulated as a concept, without projection or anachronism. For me, simply to capitulate that "race" as such did not exist yet, and that the brownness described had merely to do with class-based sun exposure, would not address the shiftiness of these constructed categories. Furthermore, there were also moments of undeniable racialization, such as a passage in Commerson's journal in which he describes the costume of sailors enacting a hazing ritual as being "decorated with feathers" and "covered with soot." He does not specifically articulate a racialized projection of indigeneity or blackness, but instead calls them "devils" and "Neptune's children." In your book *Black on Both Sides: A Racial History of Trans Identity* I felt that you were embarking on a delicate process of speaking about gendered and racialized identities—historical and contemporary—revealing a broken interwoven net, and it made me wonder how you think about the question/problem of anachronism?

C. RILEY SNORTON: I remember your presentation at the symposium as well.[1] I was really fascinated by the breadth of your research practice and how the racial histories of materials have become part of your art. In some ways, it made me think of one of the key connections I was making in the first two chapters of *Black on Both Sides*, about racialized gender and the indefatigable uses of matter. Sara Ahmed's work on related questions about racial matter and use has been illuminating.[2] Slavery functioned by rendering persons into property; the understanding of slaves as fungible fundamentally shaped both science and social perceptions of blackness as devoid of normative personal characteristics. Following Spillers's analysis in her noted essay "Mama's Baby, Papa's Maybe: An American Grammar Book," I read the distinction between flesh and body as a productive political relation that not only speaks to questions about the construction of human/non-human but also about how race (and the idea of racial difference) stages and gives language to the scientific production of sex and the historical production of gender (fig. 1). Dr. J. Marion Sims's brutal experiments on enslaved "subjects" illustrates these points, as does the history of the visual culture of gynecology. In the case of the Crafts, this was a critical context for fugitive action, leading Ellen (who "became" a disabled white slave owner) and many others to make their bodies into other beings or things. Your research and work on porcelain also speaks to how racial matter (and racializing/racializable matter) becomes the substance of ontological difference.

In terms of the question of anachronism, I pursue historical materials with an emphasis on the lineage and legacy of ideas. Having not been trained as a historian, I am more persuaded by the genealogical approach, which I was first

1 . . . . . The symposium referenced was the "New World Orders: Coloniality, Racial Intimacies, and Disability," organized by Hentyle Yapp at New York University, Jan 27, 2017. This dialogue took place in fall 2018 and was adapted by Lin and Snorton for publication.

2 . . . . . Following her study *Living a Feminist Life* (Durham, NC: Duke University Press, 2017), Sara Ahmed's forthcoming project speaks directly to questions of matter of race, diversity, and their utilities. See her summary "The Uses of Use," author website, accessed September 13, 2018, https://www.saranahmed.com/the-uses-of-use/, and her particularly helpful (or perhaps useful) post on her research blog explaining these dynamics/relations: "Institutional as Usual," October 24, 2017, https://feministkilljoys.com/2017/10/24/institutional-as-usual/.

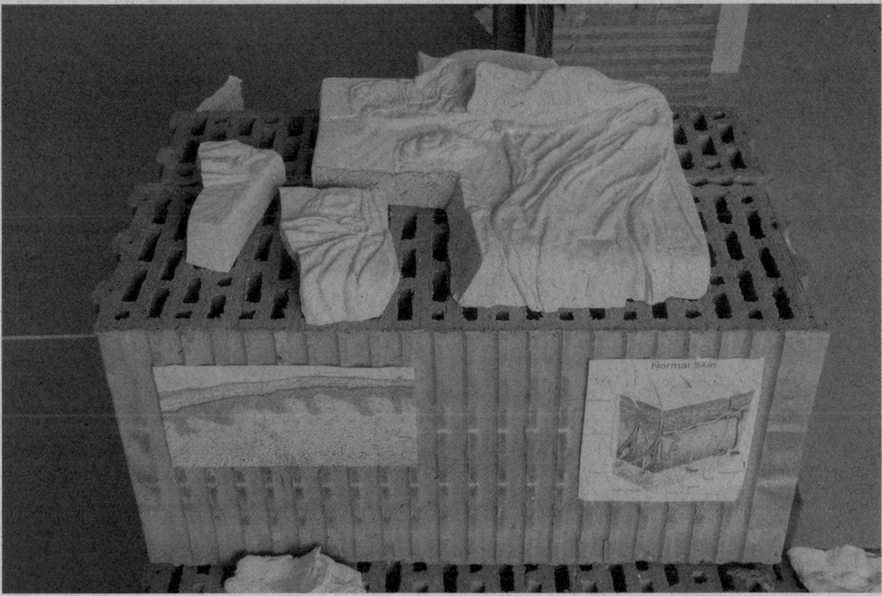

Fig. 1
Porcelain sculpture based on Sedat Pakay's photograph of James Baldwin sleeping in a bed in Istanbul in A Hard White Body, a Soft White Worm, Portikus, Frankfurt am Main, 2018

introduced to in the work of Michel Foucault.[3] But allow me to respond to your question in a slightly different way—one that reflects on your art and research practice. Part of what you do and how you do your work makes me think about the various ways we manipulate materials. I notice that you often use ancient methods/procedures to make your art. To work in this way emphasizes how many choices you/we have in working with matter, as it also underlines how technology, or so-called innovation, often betrays an underlying logic. Focusing on matter becomes a way to complicate and question some of the popular assumptions about history, a program of study that tracks change over time. Attention to materials and material praxis unsettles the common sense of time as linear, as it also reveals many of the constitutive problems of historical narration and the possibility of refusing the past as a mere instantiation of the inevitability of the present.

CL: Yes, yes! I am so interested in how technology, or innovation betrays an underlying logic, as you say. I remember reading Ian Hacking's book *Mad Travelers: Reflections on the Reality of Transient Mental Illness*, where he speculates that the diseases appearing at particular times often reflect contemporaneous anxieties and technologies. In my research on porcelain I also touched upon the history of glass and learned that King Charles VI sometimes believed he was made of glass and had himself swaddled in heavy blankets to keep from breaking. Glass production was beginning to be available to the masses then, and glass was sometimes even used to "capture" the magical aura of religious relics. Notably, the craze for porcelain was described as *Porzellankrankheit*, or porcelain sickness, a disorder marked by contagious, uncontrollable compulsion. In this older world view, agency is shifted because seemingly inanimate materials radiate and contaminate other matter through proximity, influencing and changing the behavior of animate materials—i.e., humans.

I am very interested in what you are saying about the perceived thingness of enslaved people giving rise to a perceptual fungibility where a kind of self-fashioning

3 . . . . . Michel Foucault, drawing on Friedrich Nietzsche's work on genealogy, explores this across his oeuvre, including in his four-volume study *The History of Sexuality* (1984), *The Order of Things: An Archaeology of the Human Sciences* (1966), and *The Archaeology of Knowledge* (1969).

becomes possible as an idea. This is fascinating to me because it seems to parallel a kind of liberal humanist idea of the self, but coming from very opposite circumstances and motivations. I had previously been thinking about the animistic or radiant properties of inanimate matter, or matter we socially and culturally think of as insignificant, as a way to question the idea of possessive individualism. I had wanted to think about viruses, parasites, insects, or seeds—or the desire elicited by inanimate, human-made materials like glass or porcelain—as a way to decenter the human as protagonist and thus shift the possible narratives. I think there is something in the "non-human" that not only destabilizes the liberal huMan project but also points to inaccessible histories with both opacity and palpability—making undeniable these realities without the easy resolution of transparency or accessibility. What are the ways you are thinking about how "non-human" operates, and are they related to how you activate material and often inanimate histories?

CRS: The liberal huMan project is an incoherent and insidiously convenient narrative. In much of her work Sylvia Wynter makes clear how Man is a political construction that changes over time. For her, and I tend to agree, we would be better off understanding "human" as a verb rather than a noun. Your turn to the "non-human" as sites that disrupt or at least reveal the mythos of agential, rational Man makes a lot of sense to me, as it also gestures toward a different, though not incompatible, critique of the huMan project. Strikingly, both approaches highlight the difficulty of knowing something by sight. The histories of porcelain and glass illustrate how the properties of materials can be imperceptible (and perhaps all the more dangerous because they are opaque). Intersecting histories of the transatlantic slave trade, colonialism, and their rationalizing epistemes are simply a few routes that convey how race became the visualizing logic used to distinguish Man from his others. Denise Ferreira da Silva's work is also helpful in pointing to how history and science produce Man (and his others) and necessitate and produce race as a concept developed to maintain the legitimacy of Man (and his others, through the logic of multicultural inclusion).

While not the same conversation per se, discourses about the huMan, the subject, and their non-/human others has for me precipitated a set of related questions about the problems of attributing (human) action to reason or will. In other words, after postmodernism, post-structuralism, and the death of the author, what does "agency" index exactly? I am still persuaded by Fred Moten's gesture in *In the Break*—that there is something worthwhile in reading the resistance of an object. But it's not "resistance" in the sense of an actor choosing to disrupt something so much as it is an act/the fact of being an object that in a particular time and place enables escape from the contemporaneous epistemological frame.

In our collaborative talk at the University of California, Davis, I was keenly aware of how material histories and the histories of materials reveal the "art" of science. The use of sheets in picturing gynecology conformed to the logic of portraying an object defined by negative space, which is also a way of framing the terrain of permissible sight (and thought) (fig. 2). This, I think, sharpens our shared interest in floods and flooding. Recently, I have been thinking about swamps as sites of excessive, often predatory, life. Their appearance in narratives of national founding, of precarious liberty, of transformation fascinates me, as does their materiality as terra unfirma—ground that is neither land nor water but both. Will you tell me more about your choice to flood part of the exhibition at the Logan Center for the Arts (p. 105)?

CL: I'm very interested in your notion of the "resistance of an object" as not just a simple shift in agency but, more importantly, a shift in time. There is something elusive about the physical properties of non-human matter that also interests me. It is, in a way, "timeless," though of course affected by the histories it is laden with. Which is maybe why I work with materials that have a long historical use that extends back in time, because I am interested in the lineage of these epistemological breaks—where language around the material reveals something about the human/non-human relationship in the way it is overburdened with emotion, anthropomorphism, and aura beyond the object's economic, practical, or social value. But the material itself does have, I believe, a kind of opacity (both

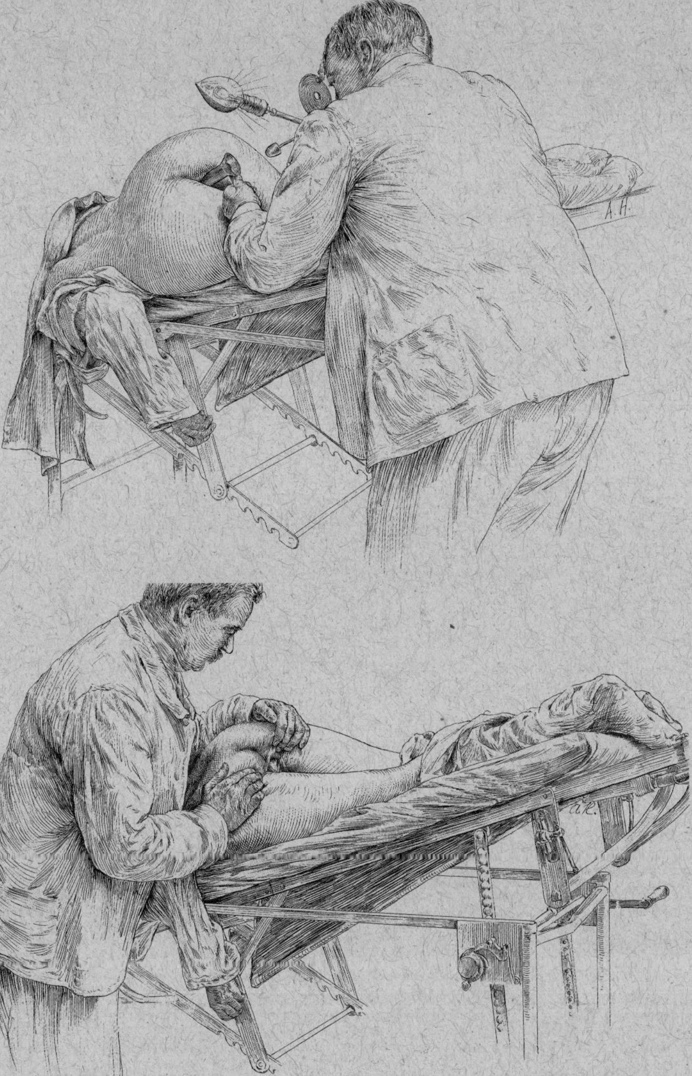

Fig. 2
Illustrations of Dr. J. Marion Sim's position for vaginal examination in Howard A. Kelly's **Medical Gynecology** (1912)

An original illustration from the Woman's Clinic Collection is in the Max Brödel Archives, in the Department of Art as Applied Medicine, The Johns Hopkins University School of Medicine, Baltimore

in the object-oriented sense and in Édouard Glissant's sense of the term). Perhaps this quality—this opacity or withdrawal or resistance that I feel from materials—is related to what you are addressing in your question around flooding and negative/positive space in your analysis of sheets in the history of gynecology. Spillers's notion of flesh seems related to me when we consider the sublimation of the human within the non-human material—in racialized language, but also literally, in the use of human bones—in the form of bone charcoal, used to refine sugar and, possibly, to form bone china (p. 117).[4] At issue is how the body of the nonhuman other (a category that includes humans with non-human status)—its (mis)use and disappearance—makes possible the other body's existence (the liberal project of huMan).

In the flooded pool I created for *A Hard White Body, a Porous Slip*, because the liquid is opaque and milky white from the addition of porcelain slip, it acts as a kind of sheet—selecting what the visitor is allowed to see and what remains submerged and withdrawn from knowing. The liquid is replenished periodically through a system in the other room that distills the piss of the people who work at the Logan Center and pumps it into the larger pool where it blends in seamlessly—another layer of invisible presence of collective bodies. As the water level shifts slightly, the submerged research materials (which include detailed, painstaking drawings alongside books, photos of archival material, photocopies, and plant matter preserved from the 1950s in its original colonial educational packaging) are slowly destroyed by the flood's soft but insistent, destructive, wearing-away effect.

So flooding for me is about instability as well, and a relation to positive and negative space, but also a shift in the horizon line. I'm thinking about Renaissance paintings in which the technology of linear perspective is used to underscore the importance of exalted religious figures, placing them at the center of the composition's horizon line so that all eye lines are drawn to them. It also makes me think of the shift that happens for me when you write

4 . . . . . The use of human bones in sugar refining was described by a Chinese coolie laborer in the 1873 report by China's Imperial Commissioner Chin Lan-pin. The recorded history of English bone China traces its origin back to a misinterpretation of the Chinese recipe for porcelain as including bone and flesh, a mistake that led to the use of animal, and perhaps also human, bones in ceramic experiments.

about Dr. Sims's surgical instruments. They shift the perspective and become this physicalization—a violent way to visualize the unspoken, invisible interior of examined black bodies. I think flooding creates this shift in the horizon line—not only politically, as an undeniable tangible effect of climate change, but also as an utter reframing that makes one wonder more about the subterranean that was always present but unaccounted for. I'm thinking here of Eva Hayward's comparison of a body of water to a human body, noting the temporary form water takes in response to the land masses that shape it, as well as its response to what is in the watershed, below visibility, and the ecologies entangled within the whole aquatic ecosystem.[5]

Now that I'm writing about it I feel somewhat naïve about this take. Maybe this is just a kind of positive romantic idea of a body of water, and I'm using it to recuperate the idea of a body as an ecosystem with fluid, temporary, and changing individual forms and not taking into account the violence of what is buried and subterranean, without choice. It seems almost the opposite of what you were saying about swamps as sites of precarious liberty, predatory life, and forms of nationalism. I am so curious to know more about what you mean.

CRS: Far from naïve, I find your description cum rationale incredibly compelling. Your observation about horizons of visibility is what interests me about swamps as well. I view them as sites that unsettle the terra firma logics of colonialism, Man, and the Subject and disturb the distinction between life and death or freedom and choice. I am fascinated by the constitutive presence of swamps to racial practices and formations in the Americas. Narratives about swamp people and swamp things seem to punctuate stories about the New World, from the Maroon communities constituted by formerly enslaved Africans and Native peoples beginning in the early sixteenth century to the first Asians (Filipinos) to arrive in America, who settled in swamps surrounding modern-day New Orleans in 1763. The stories of refuge-seekers who find temporary or more permanent reprieve in the swamps underscore what Neil Roberts argues is the "central maxim

5. . . . . See Cleo Woelfle-Erskine and July Cole, "Transfiguring the Anthropocene: Scholastic Reimaginings of Human-Beaver Worlds," TSQ: Transgender Studies Quarterly, special issue, Tranimalities 2, no. 2 (May 1, 2015): 297–316.

of a theory of marroonage: freedom is not a place; it is a state of being," but the relationships between place and being—while not fixed—are inextricably intertwined.[6] The seeming invisibility of place-being obscures the necessary relation between a metaphysics of presence and a metaphysics of place, and how ideas about "freedom" and "choice" are bound up in this relation. The swamp then becomes a rubric for reading how freedom is neither abstracted nor wholly performative but an exercise that works in and on a body—a praxis Harriet Jacobs described as "choice" when in "no situation to choose."[7]

But there is also something—if not naïve, then certainly hopeful—that I read into the material and metaphorical dimensions of swamps. They can be generative places from which to explore what Ferreira da Silva terms a "critical arsenal" for reading the production of Man "without rehearsing either the logic of discovery or the thesis of transparency."[8] I see Ferreira da Silva's work as underscoring a part of our discussion about how material is made to make sense according to existing rubrics of the huMan project—which is a paradox, precisely because that which instantiates the huMan project is also the key to its demise: being the subject/object of reason. This is perhaps what excites me most about matter being supposedly devoid of reason (and the ever-elusive question of how matter matters): its very thingliness—and here I am thinking about Bill Brown's work on how a thing doesn't really index an object, per se, but rather a set of subject-object relations—suggests a material instability that exceeds modern and postmodern epistemological frames.[9]

6 . . . . . Neil Roberts, *Freedom as Marroonage* (Chicago: University of Chicago Press, 2015), 11.

7 . . . . . Harriet Jacobs, *Incidents in the Life of a Slave Girl* (Boston: Thayer and Eldridge, 1861), 171.

8 . . . . . Denise Ferreira da Silva, *Toward a Global Idea of Race* (Minneapolis: University of Minnesota Press, 2007), xviii.

9 . . . . . Bill Brown, "Thing Theory," *Critical Inquiry* 28, no.1 (Autumn 2001): 1–22.

CANDICE LIN'S MINOR ECOLOGIES

RIZVANA BRADLEY

Candice Lin's mixed-media installations have incorporated materials and objects as varied as poppy seeds, sugar, silkworms, tea, gum tragacanth, edible pigments, candied fruits and leaves, plants, and cockroaches. Placing into ensemblic proximity the vestigial traces and scattered archives of colonialism that linger into the historical present, Lin's installations achieve an ecological balance, conveying how plant and insect species as well as rare and devalued objects become part of ephemeral archives that go largely unseen and undocumented. The miscellany of objects and discarded materials the artist displays speak to lesser-known recorded events and intellectual histories. Lin's work conveys how the trace events and figures that haunt history's minor edges are entangled with the legacies of capture and subjection that gave rise to modern forms of power.

Works like *Physiologus*, *The Worm Husband (Our Father)*, *The Roots of Industry*, and *The Tea Table*, featured in *A Body Reduced to Brilliant Colour*, Lin's 2016 exhibition at Gasworks, London, offer meticulously cataloged models, specimens, and illustrations that appear in the form of etchings or engravings (figs. 1–4). Sometimes these displays, which are also presented in leather-bound books and rectangular terrariums, offer a selection of objects, insects, and other ephemera that compose fabricated biological histories. Lin operates much like a historical materialist. In a Benjaminian sense, her practice is attentive to the way history unfolds in the present and places aesthetic emphasis on collecting, rather than on the collection of objects. But as a sustained political praxis, Lin's alternative method of collecting remains attuned to minor lives, synthesizing and simulating the chief venture of colonial modernity—the leisurely activities of acquiring and accumulating—as interwoven with legacies of conquest, plunder, and environmental waste. The objects and materials included in Lin's installations disrupt our linear sense of colonial history, its representational forms, and indexical signs. Rather than offering a detailed historical account, Lin's intertextual practice frequently works through a set of allegorical procedures. Substituting the conscripted laborer for the figure of the European in *The Roots*

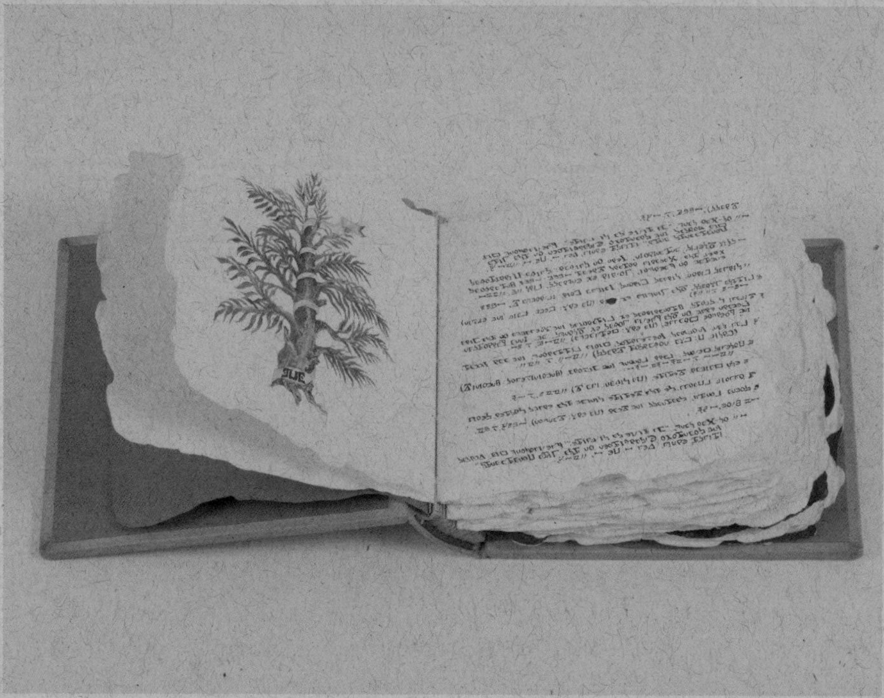

Fig. 1
Physiologus, 2016. Artist's book. Leather, watercolor, graphite, and ink on handmade paper, 17 × 16.5 cm (6¾ × 6½ in.) Binding and transcription by Joel Freeman. Commissioned by Gasworks, London

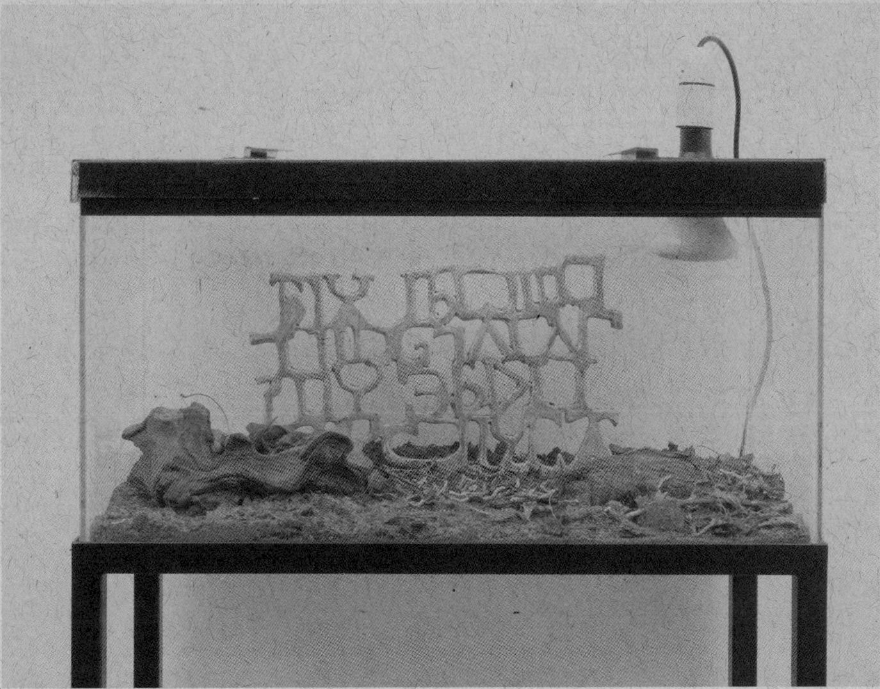

Fig. 2
The Worm Husband (Our Father), 2016.
Silkworms, tank, glazed porcelain,
plaster and heating mechanism,
and miscellaneous plant material,
150 × 61 cm (59 × 24 in.)
Commissioned by Gasworks, London

Fig. 3
The Roots of Industry, 2016.
Etching, 63.5 × 76.2 cm (25 × 30 in.)
Commissioned by Gasworks, London

Fig. 4
The Tea Table, 2016. Etching,
63.5 × 76.2 cm (25 × 30 in.)
Commissioned by Gasworks, London

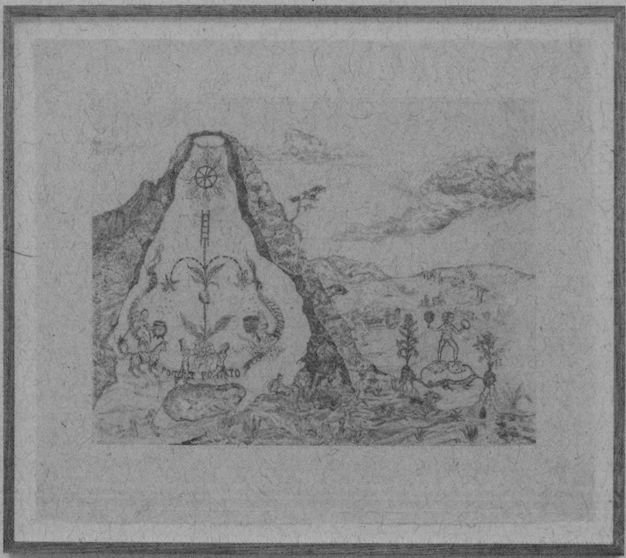

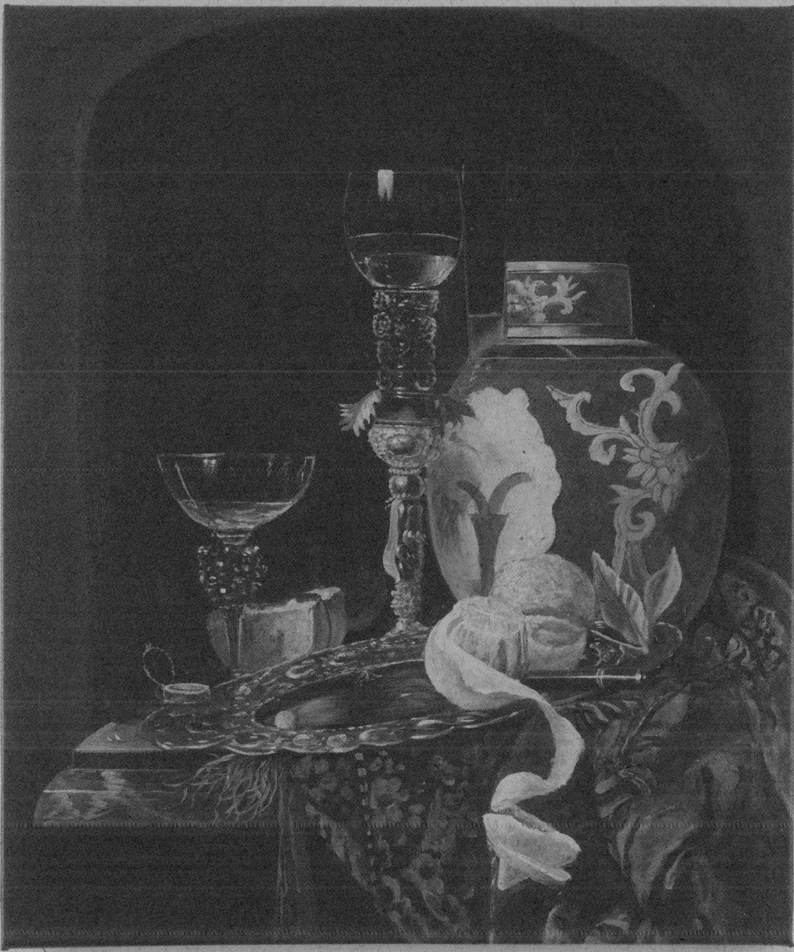

Fig. 5
Reproduction of a Reproduction, 2016. Chinese reproduction of Willem Kalf's 1669 painting **Still Life with a Chinese Porcelain Jar.** Oil on canvas, 76.2 × 66 cm (30 × 26 in.) Commissioned by Gasworks, London

of *Industry*, for example, or in *Reproduction of a Reproduction*, where the artist includes a recent Chinese-made reproduction of Willem Kalf's 1669 painting *Still Life with a Chinese Porcelain Jar*, Lin's surrogate objects and figures effectively detourn the conventional signs of colonial modernity's surfeit enjoyments (fig. 5). Such wayward substitutions and false reproductions demonstrate how colonial modernity's invention of race as a global idea[1] is linked to the production, consumption, and circulation of images and objects.

Lin's artistic practice is concerned with the latent, obscure, and contradictory histories of objects. Informed by a deconstructive methodology, her work disrupts disciplinary and institutional distinctions between researching and collecting, writing and studying, historical investigation and critical fabulation—the latter having been articulated by Saidiya Hartman as a necessary minoritarian, counter-interpretive practice. Lin's installations and their fragile landscapes place as much emphasis on researching as on making. Suspending objects in relation, Lin offers a practice of critical fabulation that entails "playing with and rearranging the basic elements of the story . . . re-presenting the sequence of events in divergent stories" in order to "jeopardize the status of the event, to displace the received or authorized account, and to imagine what might have happened or might have been said or might have been done."[2] Lin's practice of fabulation crosses art historical methodologies, expanding the material afterlife of the object and extending its dimensionality.

Following Hartman's critical interpretive method, Lin explores the archive's limits as well as its constitutive resistances. She exploits the archive's sources, revealing them as fictions of history in order to "make visible the production of disposable lives."[3] Considering Hartman alongside Fred Moten's assertion that "the category of the human has been put under the severest pressure by the terrors of colonialism and imperialism,"[4] Lin attunes us to an artistic practice that hinges on the aesthetic possibility

1. . . . . . See Denise Ferreira da Silva, *Toward a Global Idea of Race* (Minneapolis: University of Minnesota Press, 2007).
2. . . . . . Saidiya Hartman, "Venus in Two Acts," *Small Axe* 26, vol. 12, no. 2 (June 2008): 11.
3. . . . . . Ibid.
4. . . . . . Fred Moten, "Blackness and Poetry," *Evening Will Come* 55 (July 1, 2015), accessed via *Arcade: Literature, Humanities, and the World*, https://arcade.stanford.edu/content/blackness-and-poetry-0.

of recovering those disposable lives relegated to a realm outside of humanity's normative sphere, where they remain hidden in plain sight. Lin's radically horizontal sculptural landscapes betray the disposability of these lives as intertwined with the resistive legacies of objects[5] and throws into crisis the epistemological discontinuities between presumably discrete histories.

Focusing on the historical materiality of porcelain, *A Hard White Body, a Porous Slip*, Lin's recent exhibition at the Reva and David Logan Center for the Arts at the University of Chicago, conveys the artist's keen sense of the ways contemporary artistic categories have come to sustain hierarchies of aesthetic and cultural meaning (p. 105). The immaculacy of porcelain is no doubt linked to its associations with whiteness, and Lin conjures the fictional aura of purity that permeates and suffuses its glossy, smooth materiality. But porcelain's glassy, polished surface proves deceptive in this regard, as Lin presents us with a porcelain slip, a liquid mixture of clay and other materials suspended in water. The work calls our attention not to the object but to the complex, multifarious process that informs its making. Lin is less interested in porcelain's unblemished surface than in the admixture that lends itself to the process of casting and shaping objects. Rather than presenting the consistency of the material's surface aesthetics, this work is interested in the gravity and viscosity of objects suspended in relation to one another. Subsequently, Lin is interested in history's temporal suspension. Much in the same way that Gilles Deleuze and Felix Guattari imagined "smooth space"[6] as non-homogenous, inherently heterogeneous, and teeming with intensity and material differentiation, for Lin, porcelain's smooth, porous slip is materially elastic, dense, and viscous and renders visible the connections between art, ethnography, and history's disposable figures. In working with porcelain in this way, Lin recasts a visual sensorium in which its smooth surface signifies not as the immaculate white foil for cultural otherness (a status readily perceived in the nineteenth century) but as an unconventional vessel for touching

5. . . . . . Ibid.

6. . . . . . See Gilles Deleuze and Felix Guattari, *A Thousand Plateaus: Capitalism and Schizophrenia* (Minneapolis: University of Minnesota Press, 1987).

and sensing marginalized lives and histories that remain partially submerged.

A Hard White Body, a Porous Slip brings together figures as distinct as the twentieth-century writer and critic James Baldwin, the eighteenth-century botanist Jeanne Baret, and the early eighteenth-century naturalist Maria Sibylla Merian. There is a resonance between the sculptural installation of a bedroom made of unfired porcelain that refers to Baldwin's second novel, *Giovanni's Room*, and the free-floating objects Lin incorporates within that space, which sink, resurface, and touch photographs, archival documents, and other literary ephemera. The work conveys a sense of disparate histories broken, severed, and re-stitched in order to be pieced together again. Furthermore, this impure setting for the viewing and discovery of the art object lends itself to an ongoing practice of fabulation. Lin demonstrates how, paradoxically, the appeal and pristine allure of porcelain is presented in a highly contaminated aesthetic environment. For instance, when *A Hard White Body* was installed at Bétonsalon – Center for Art and Research, Paris, Lin presented a bedroom inspired by Baldwin's novel that was moistened with a distillation of piss, water from the Seine, and plants that referenced Baret's research (p. 45).

At the Logan Center, Lin evokes the historical presence of porcelain at the 1893 World's Columbian Exposition in Chicago, which incorporated racialized caricatures of blacks and Native Americans in commercial displays for American products sold overseas. Establishing ethnographic artifacts as functioning artistic displays, the exposition was a cultural exercise in empire building that helped legitimize American economic imperialism. Alluding to the geographic closeness of the Chicago exposition and the Logan Center, Lin's installation collapses their historical separation and proposes that the shared institutional grammars of collecting and display are more porous than we might think. She exposes the connections between the allure of porcelain at the world's fair and the matrix of valuation that historically has accrued to raced and gendered bodies subjected to injury and violation. But Lin also structures her practice around a concern for the submerged desires and pleasures that inform minor embodied histories. The play of elements in these installations negotiates the contingency of the legacies of erasure and fugitive resistance to it, which could be said to have preceded the violence of colonial and imperial expropriation.

More generally, in Lin's practice the ongoing contamination of art by ethnography and of ethnography by art is bound up with the revelation of the inherent fragility of the disciplinary boundaries between the two. Experimenting with these divides by contaminating them, the artist consistently undermines the enforced distinctions between epistemologies that inform how we think about the production and circulation of cultural objects. In this way, her practice invokes James Clifford's argument for retrospectively cutting across the established definitions of modernist art and ethnographic study. In his essay "On Ethnographic Surrealism" Clifford advocates for "recaptur[ing] a situation in which ethnography is again something unfamiliar and surrealism [is] not a bounded province of art and literature."[7] He deploys an expanded definition of the surreal "to circumscribe an esthetic that values fragments, curious collections, unexpected juxtapositions." Drawing upon Susan Sontag, Clifford offers a more capacious understanding of surrealism and its function within culture more broadly, arguing that surrealism ought to be viewed as a "pervasive, dominant modern sensibility," a "set of attitudes" irreducible to a specific aesthetic movement or art historical canon.[8]

Crossing, polluting, and linking seemingly disparate modernist histories is central to Lin's practice. The porous liquid slip brings together Baldwin's twentieth-century critique of the aestheticization of a universalizing whiteness (which functions doubly as a critique of whiteness's aesthetic autonomy) with the naturalist sensitivities of Baret and Merian in order to stake an intervention in the imperial ethnographic legacies of modernism that are based on precise distributions of power. A concern with the entanglement of the object's colonial history and its erotic potentiality is reflected in the dirt that accrues to the archival documents Lin resources. But these materials also evoke the retrospective obscuring of violence, power, and histories of subjection that informed the ethnographic

7. . . . . . James Clifford, "On Ethnographic Surrealism," Comparative Studies in Society and History 23, no. 4 (October 1981): 539.

8. . . . . . Ibid., 540.

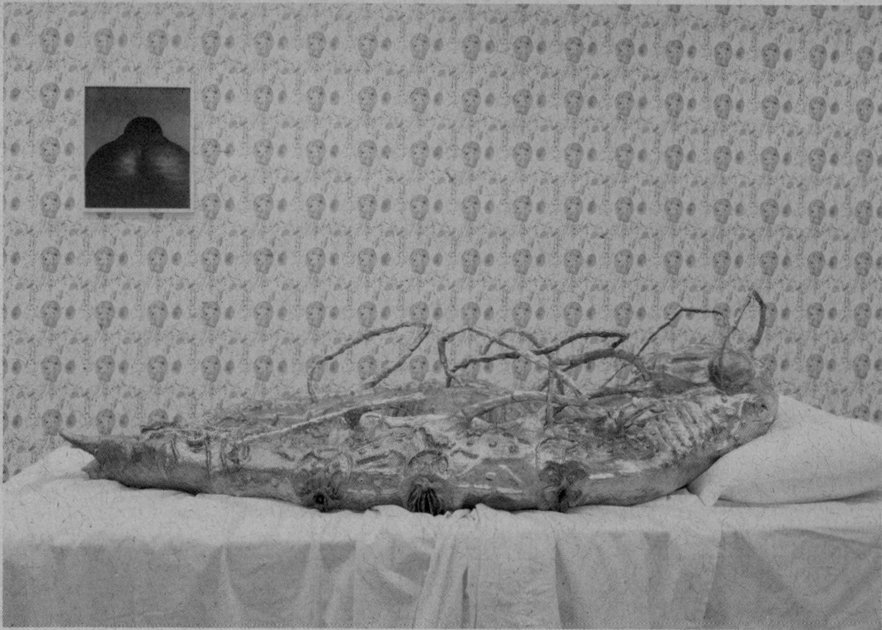

Fig. 6
Installation view of The long-lasting intimacy of strangers, Galeria Quadrado Azul, Porto, Portugal, 2013. Courtesy the artist, Galeria Quadrado Azul, Porto, and François Ghebaly, Los Angeles

constructions of difference on which modernist aesthetic categories and hierarchies were founded.

Lin's method for resourcing objects and materials betrays what Clifford refers to as a "crucial ethnographic attitude."[9] As in the 2013 work *The long-lasting intimacy of strangers*, the fragmented topography of Lin's installations, which reimagine insect and bacterial ecologies, blends a beautiful and complex mix of references while confronting us with an understanding of our own historical culpabilities: our erosive and corrosive techniques of environmental sabotage (fig. 6). Our material realities are not pre-given, natural, and familiar but are composed of different orders and arrangements of meaning. Lin's layered, compositional practice imagines connections between disparate cultural and political sensibilities while threading together impermanent archives, enabling us to see the artist working beyond the project of recovering the transparent truth of racial and gender inequalities. Revealing the boundaries between art and science to be tenuous and even fluid, Lin brings the fact of their porosity to bear on the production of culture and the practice of history.

If ethnography has been methodologically informed by the study of difference between empire and its colonies, it also has been embedded in forms of scientific inquiry obsessed with the notion of first discovery. As Clifford puts it: "If the boundaries between art and science . . . are ideological and shifting . . . [the] changing definitions of art or science must provoke new retrospective unities, new ideal types for historical description."[10] Lin's surreal juxtapositions expose the intimate connections between science and empire while recuperating an alternative ethnographic method concerned with deconstructing colonial networks of collecting and exchange. The speculative and improvisational, cross-historical dialogues between Baldwin, Baret, and Merian imagine a porous relationship between art and science, bringing them into closer proximity with surreal ethnography as open-ended praxis.

Lin's installations link the reification of nature to the commodificiation of objects. In this regard, her work conveys a sustained interest in the way our knowledge of

9. . . . . . Ibid., 541

10. . . . . . Ibid.

nature is bound up with the lesser-known histories of deviant natural forms. How, for example, does eighteenth-century naturalism account for the forms of plant life and organic material that were intricately linked with slave resistance in that period? Asking such questions in works like *System for a Stain* (2016) and *La Charada China* (2018), for example, approaches a practice of surreal ethnography that hews closely to the act of critical fabulation and furthermore speaks to the lingering connections between slavery, modernity, and contemporary global trade structures (figs. 7 and 8). Transposed to the realm of praxis, the retrospective turn to cultural artifacts detached from their sources of origin and reorganized and re-circulated through other systems of meaning constitutes a dialectical activity of "render[ing] the unfamiliar comprehensible" and "making the familiar strange."[11]

Relating the lesser-known material archives of botanical collectors to naturalism's role in the development of colonial knowledge, Lin improvises through scientific ideas about human and nonhuman difference from the eighteenth century through the present. Such a practice of discovery and disruption calls our attention to the nature of race, gender, and sexual difference as analytic categories fashioned and constructed at the intersections of these more obscure colonial contexts. Lin reactivates ephemeral archives that interrogate the historical circumscription of scientific and aesthetic knowledge. Simultaneously, her work retrospectively rediscovers entanglements of culture and nature, revealing the ways human and nonhuman lives are enfolded.

Demonstrating how empire and science developed in parallel, Lin conveys a certain resistance to the established methods of ethnographic research by revealing how the quotidian life of objects and their attendant histories of circulation uncover other possible forms of relation. For Lin, the imagined dialogues between Baldwin, Merian, and Baret establish these figures as minor actants in a network that places emphasis on ontological and metaphysical distinctions rather than simply on sociological differences. This argument, elaborated in the critical sociology of Bruno Latour, lets us view the mixed-media ecology of Lin's installation as an assemblage of human and nonhuman

11. . . . . . Ibid., 542.

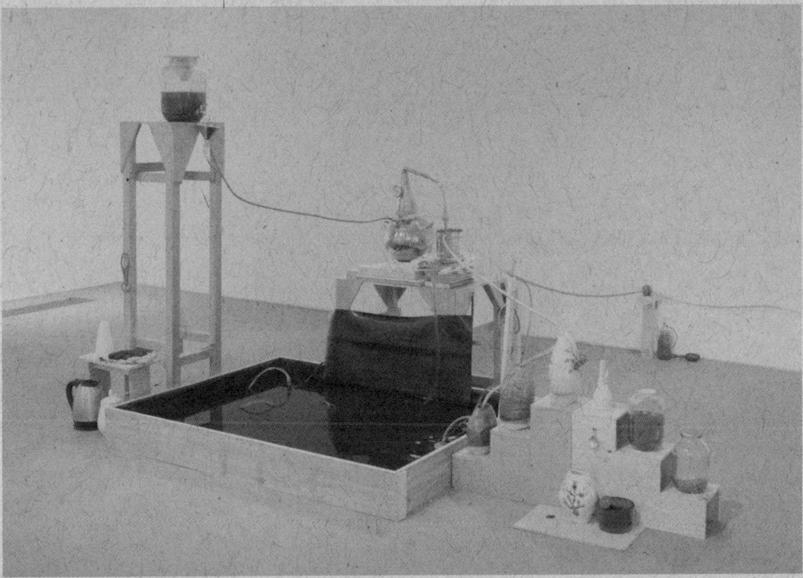

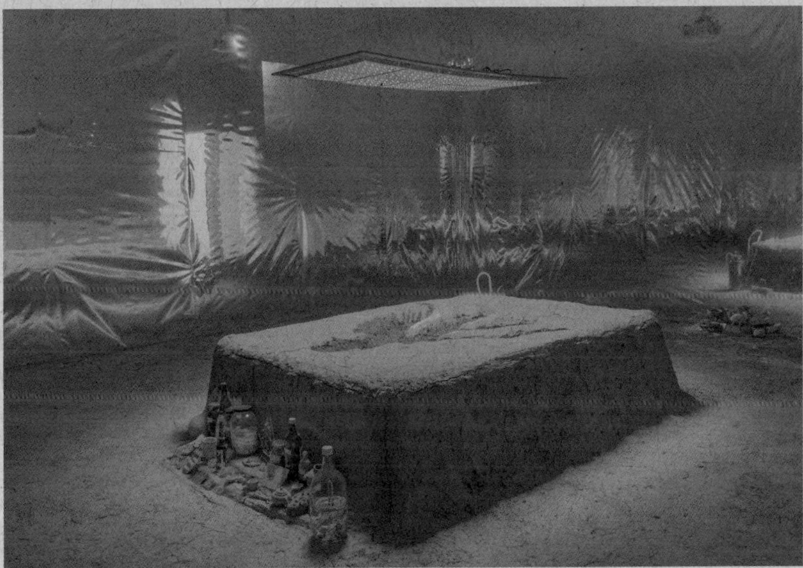

Fig 7
System for a Stain, 2016. Wood, glass jars, cochineal, poppy seeds, metal castings, water, tea, sugar, copper still, hot plate, ceramic vessels, mortar and pestle, mud from the Thames, jar, microbial mud battery, and vinyl floor, dimensions variable. Commissioned by Gasworks, London

Fig 8
La Charada China, 2018. Installation view from the Taipei Biennial, 2018

agencies. Her porcelain slip fashions an aesthetic network whose structure is irreducible "to human individual actors" and "extend[s] the word actor—or actant—to nonhuman, non individual entities."[12]

Like much of Lin's repertoire, *A Hard White Body, a Porous Slip* presents us with an interwoven set of material references, a web of human life enmeshed with a dazzling assemblage of vital matter that potentially complicates our sense of what constitutes an aesthetic environment. Philosopher and theorist Jane Bennett has argued for the interdependency of humans and objects. Offering a process-oriented materialism that elaborates a concept of distributive agency, Bennett's vital theory of objects deconstructs the notion of human intentionality, insisting that agency is more complexly extended through nonhuman actants. Bennett further claims that agency "involves not mere motion . . . where motion is willed or intended by a subject." Focusing instead on what she identifies as "a swarm of vitalities at play," Bennett recognizes "human intentions as always in competition or confederation with many other strivings."[13] Lin's porcelain slip aestheticizes the variously positioned strivings of minor actants across dispersed histories. Realizing the compression of philosophical and material histories as a speculative ecology of aesthetic forms, Lin's repertoire metabolizes the full complexity of what we might call an ecopoetics. By consistently combining artifacts and histories that would not conventionally be associated in reality, Lin produces a surreal ecology and, in so doing, improvises on the distinction between an ecopolitics and an ecopoetics, where the latter offers an opening into social and ecological life and gestures toward ecopoetical figurations that exceed what empire can envision.[14]

12. . . . . . Bruno Latour, *Re-Assembling the Social: An Introduction to Actor-Network Theory* (Oxford, UK: Oxford University Press, 2005), 2.
13. . . . . . Jane Bennett, *Vibrant Matter: A Political Ecology of Things* (Durham, NC: Duke University Press, 2010), 31–32.
14. . . . . . Angela Hume and Gillian Osborne, eds. *Ecopoetics: Essays in the Field* (Iowa City: University of Iowa Press, 2018), 149.

PORTIKUS, FRANKFURT AM MAIN

PAGES 77–90
INSTALLATION VIEWS OF
A HARD WHITE BODY,
A SOFT WHITE WORM

FEBRUARY 10–APRIL 8, 2018

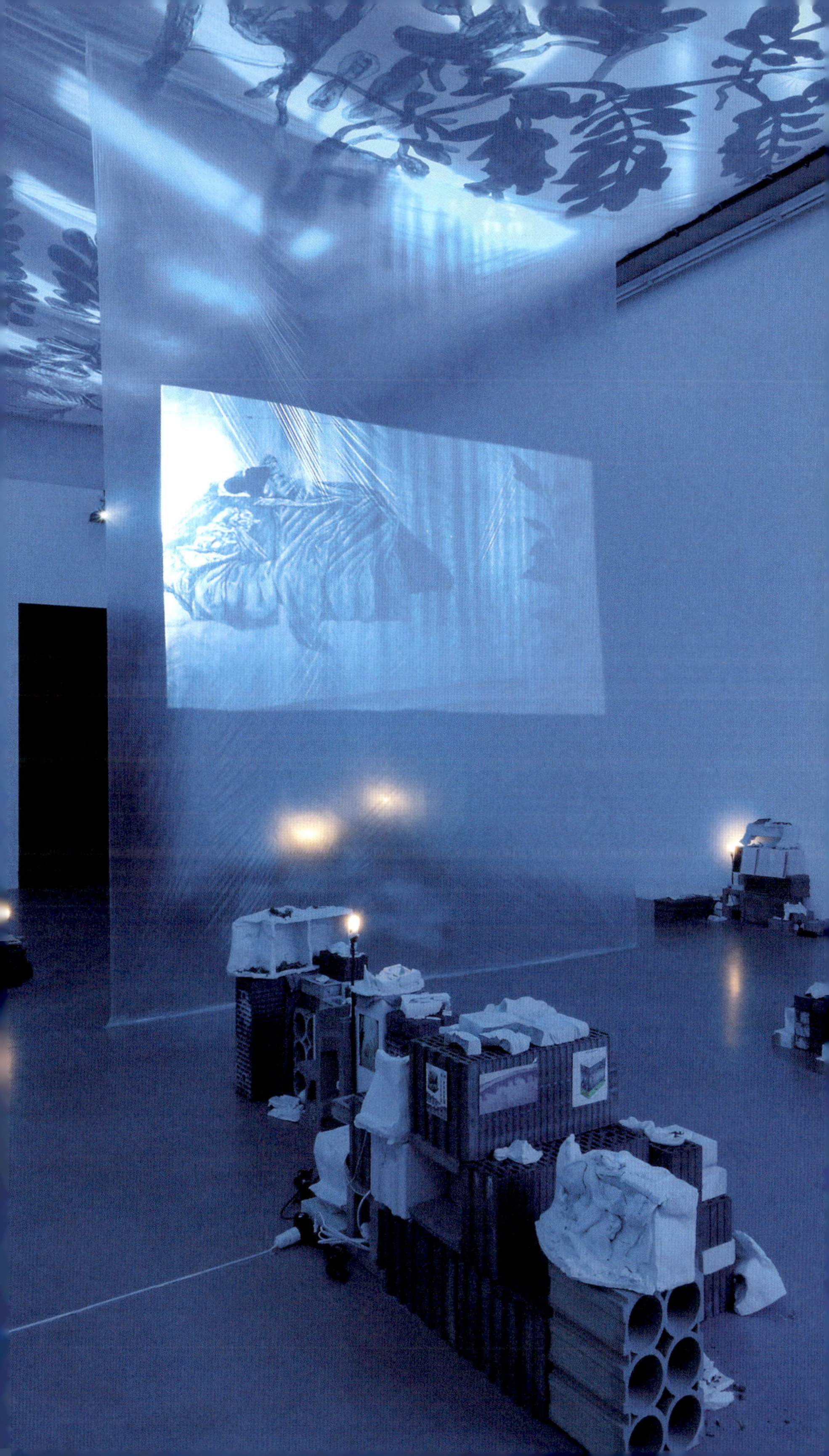

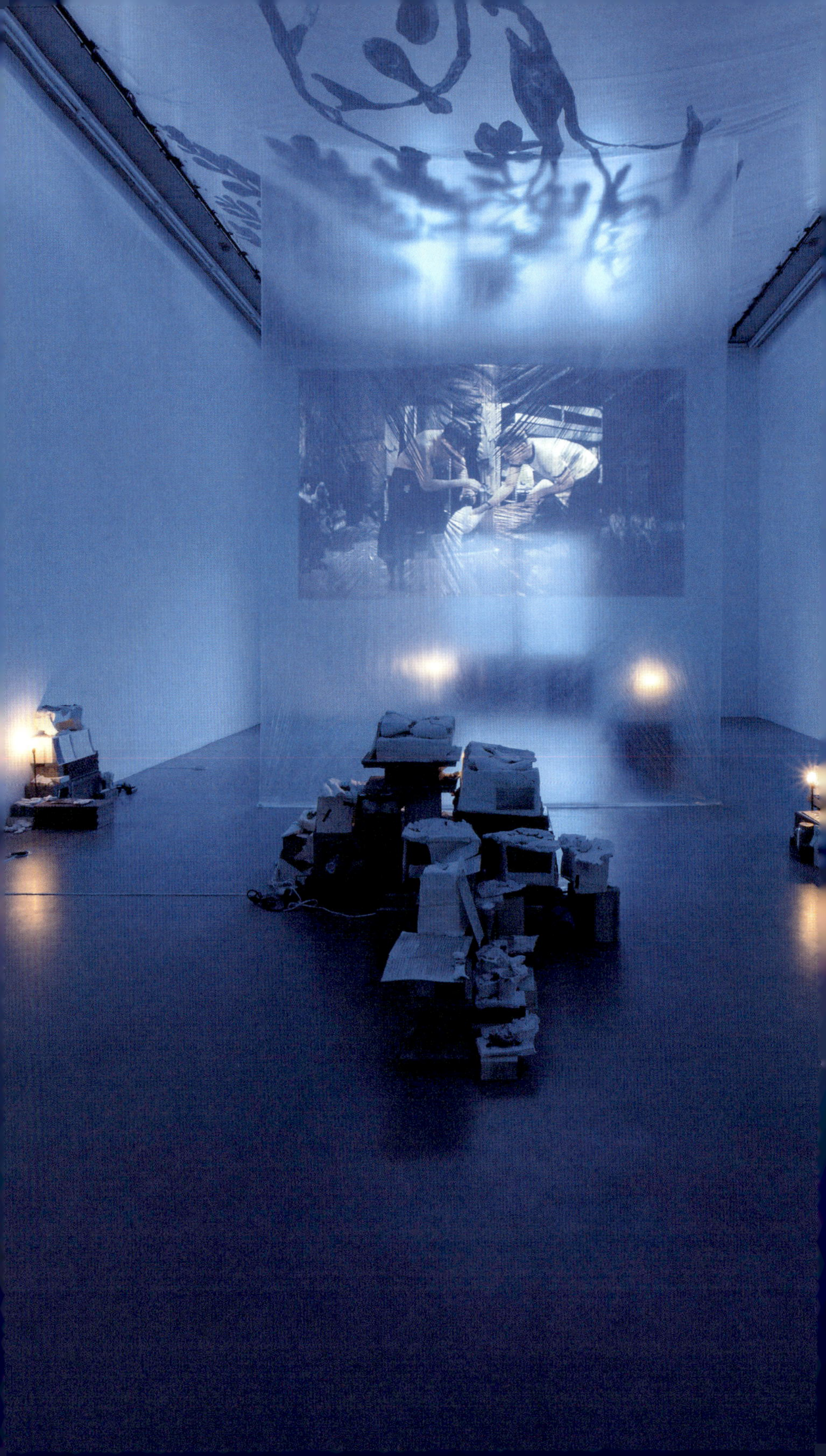

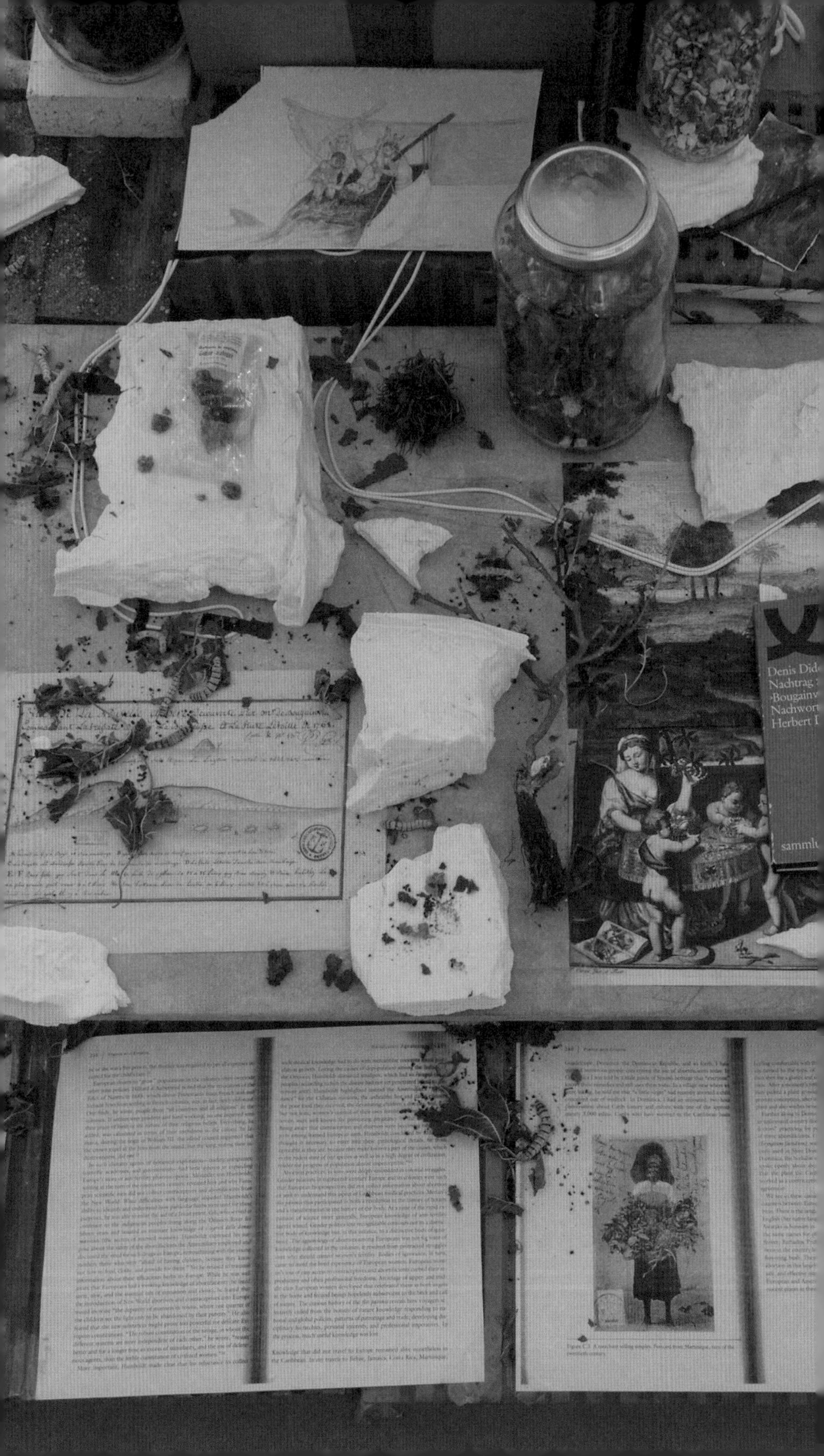

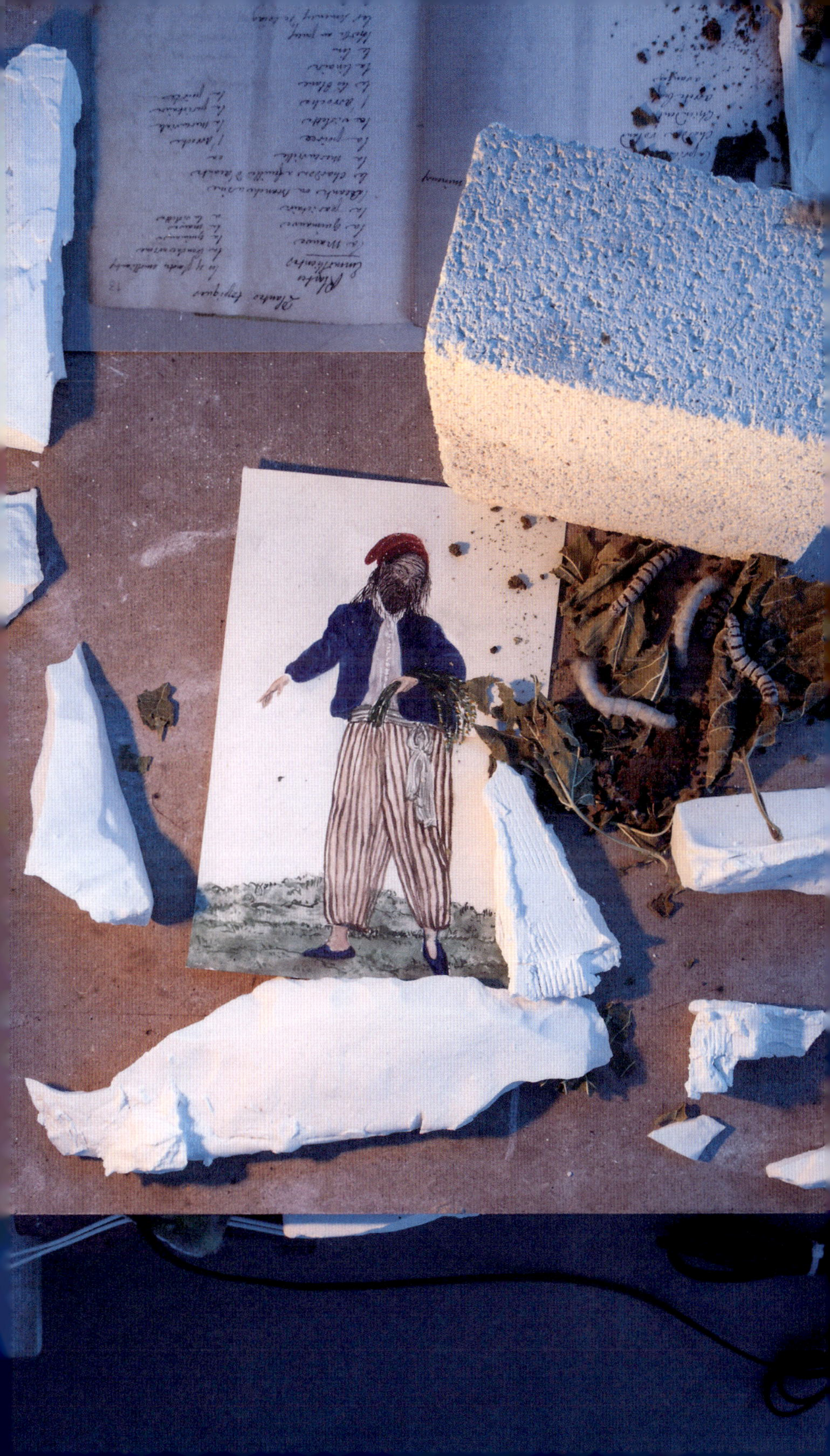

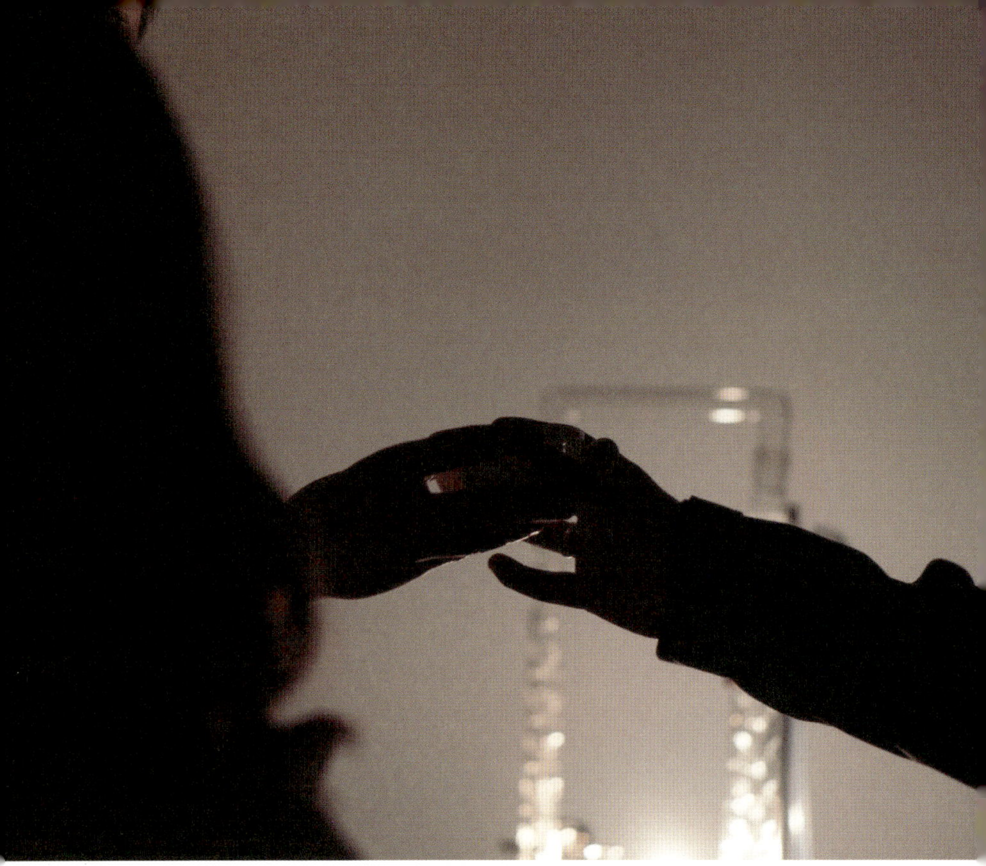

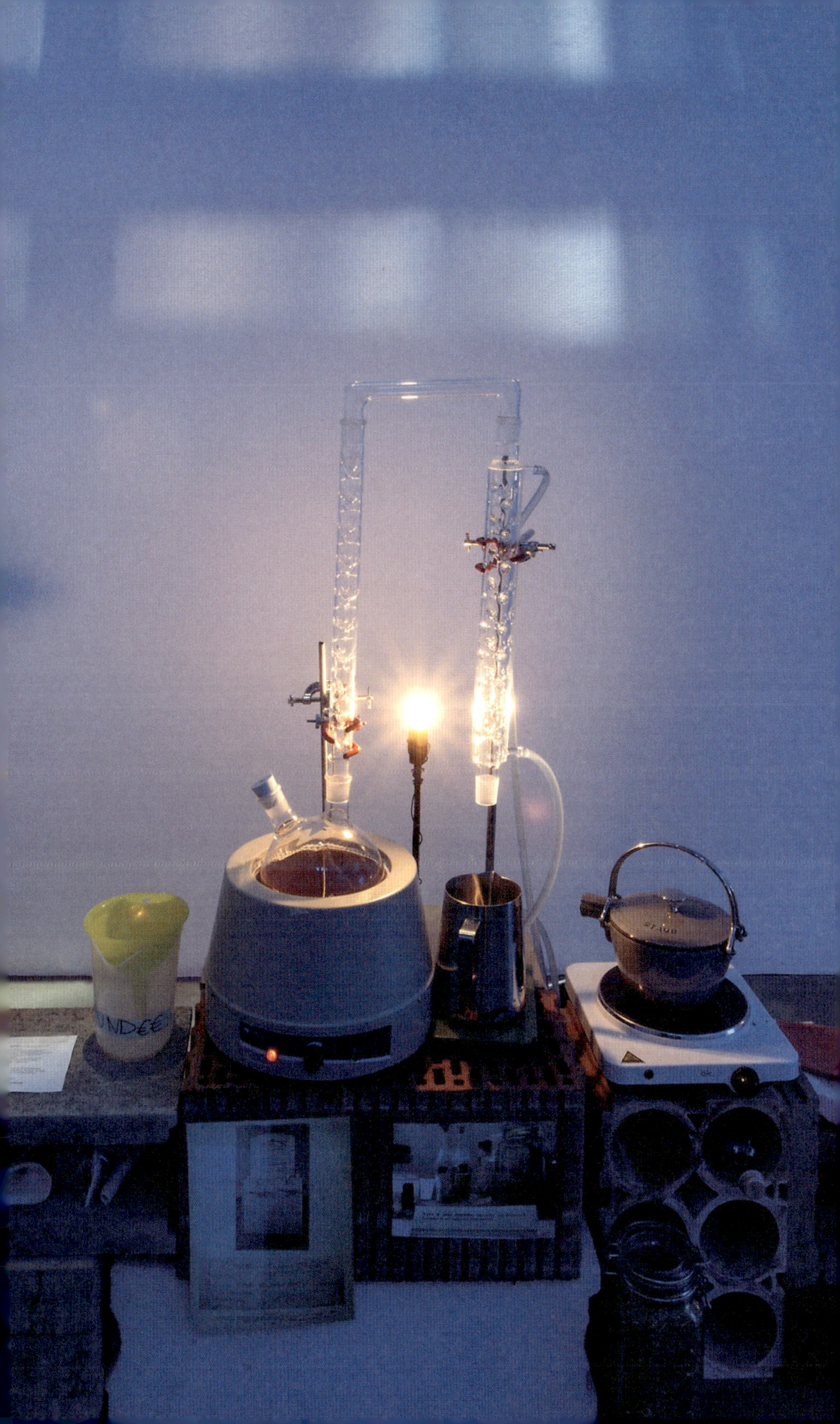

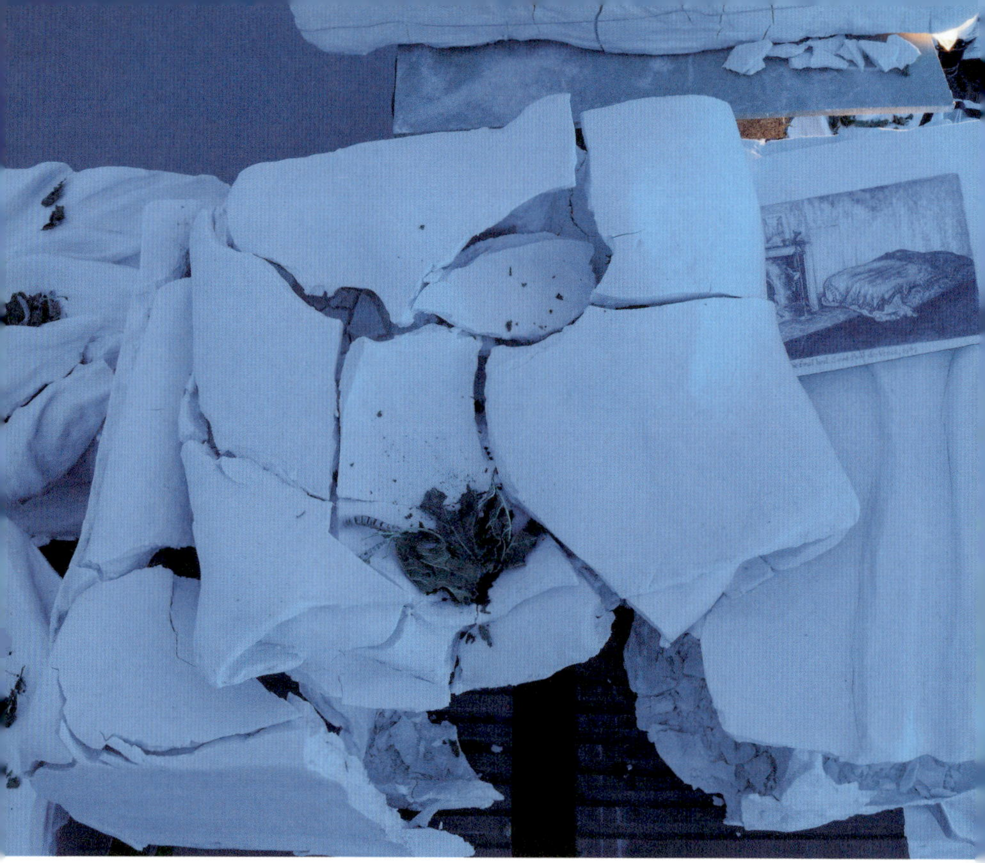

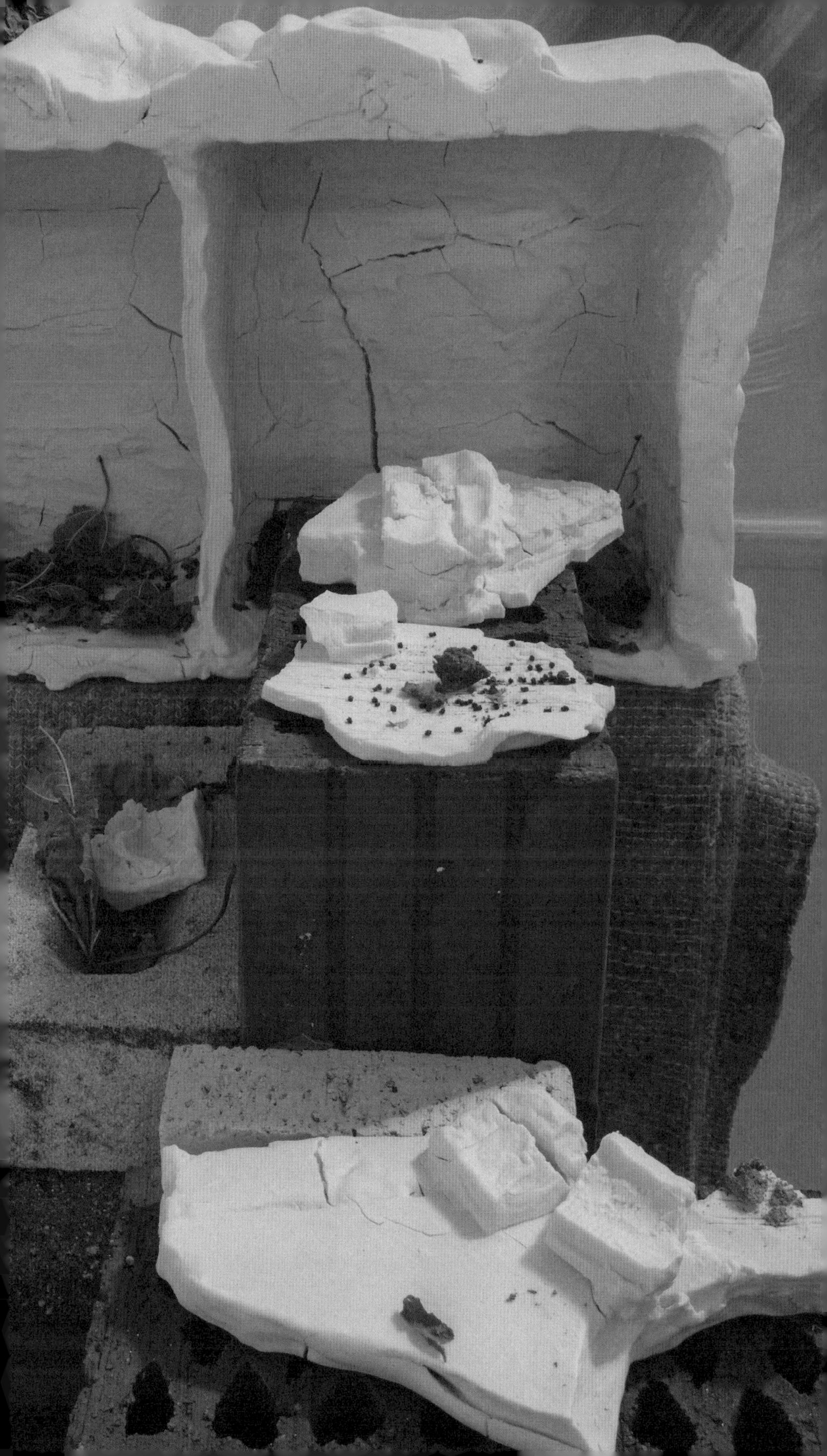

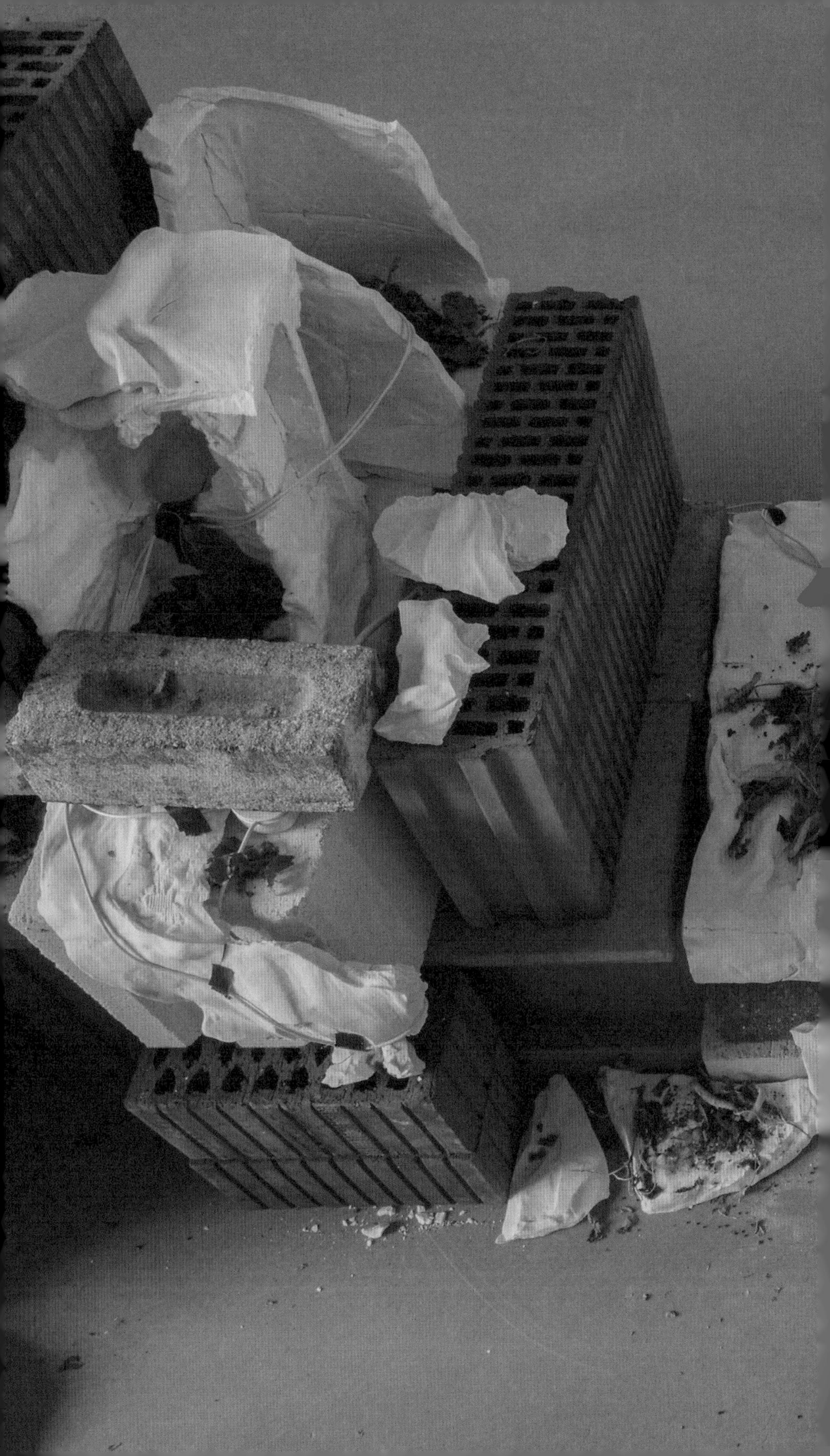

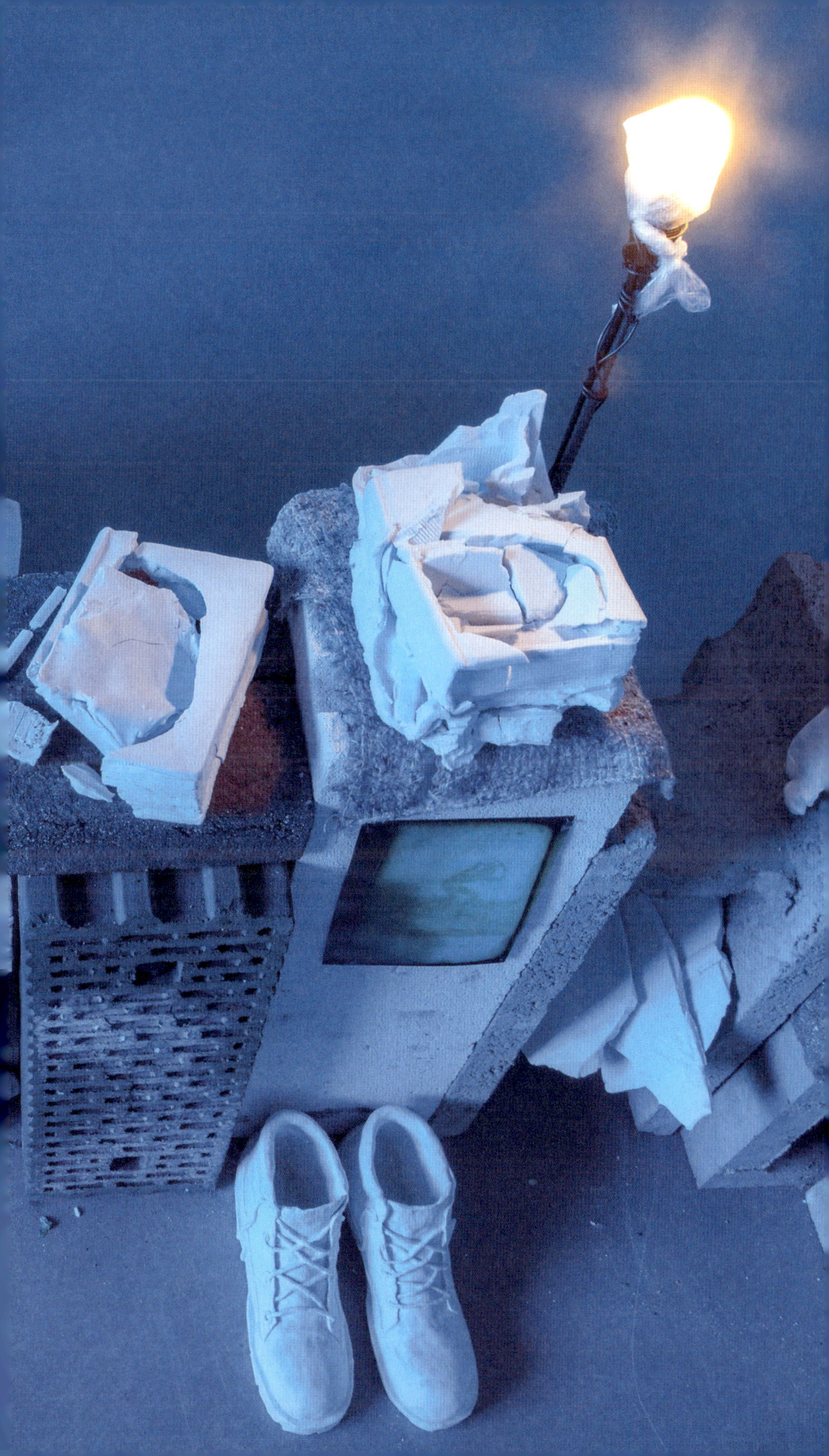

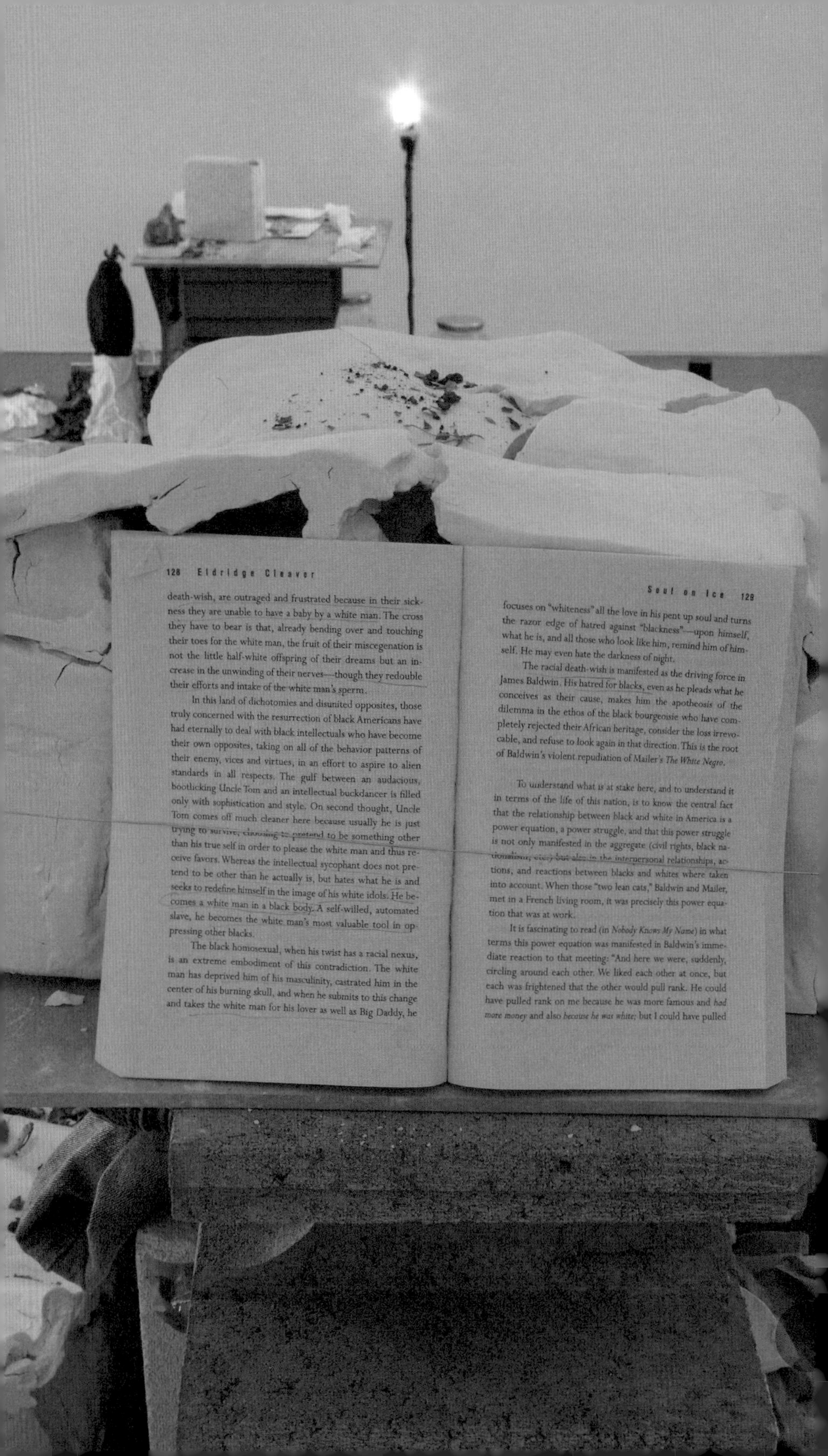

128 Eldridge Cleaver
death-wish, are outraged and frustrated because in their sick-
ness they are unable to have a baby by a white man. The cross
they have to bear is that, already bending over and touching
their toes for the white man, the fruit of their miscegenation is
not the little half-white offspring of their dreams but an in-
crease in the unwinding of their nerves—though they redouble
their efforts and intake of the white man's sperm.
In this land of dichotomies and disunited opposites, those
truly concerned with the resurrection of black Americans have
had eternally to deal with black intellectuals who have become
their own opposites, taking on all of the behavior patterns of
their enemy, vices and virtues, in an effort to aspire to alien
standards in all respects. The gulf between an audacious,
bootlicking Uncle Tom and an intellectual buckdancer is filled
only with sophistication and style. On second thought, Uncle
Tom comes off much cleaner here because usually he is just
trying to survive, choosing to pretend to be something other
than his true self in order to please the white man and thus re-
ceive favors. Whereas the intellectual sycophant does not pre-
tend to be other than he actually is, but hates what he is and
seeks to redefine himself in the image of his white idols. He be-
comes a white man in a black body. A self-willed, automated
slave, he becomes the white man's most valuable tool in op-
pressing other blacks.
The black homosexual, when his twist has a racial nexus,
is an extreme embodiment of this contradiction. The white
man has deprived him of his masculinity, castrated him in the
center of his burning skull, and when he submits to this change
and takes the white man for his lover as well as Big Daddy, he
Soul on Ice 129
focuses on "whiteness" all the love in his pent up soul and turns
the razor edge of hatred against "blackness"—upon himself,
what he is, and all those who look like him, remind him of him-
self. He may even hate the darkness of night.
The racial death-wish is manifested as the driving force in
James Baldwin. His hatred for blacks, even as he pleads what he
conceives as their cause, makes him the apotheosis of the
dilemma in the ethos of the black bourgeoisie who have com-
pletely rejected their African heritage, consider the loss irrevo-
cable, and refuse to look again in that direction. This is the root
of Baldwin's violent repudiation of Mailer's *The White Negro*.
To understand what is at stake here, and to understand it
in terms of the life of this nation, is to know the central fact
that the relationship between black and white in America is a
power equation, a power struggle, and that this power struggle
is not only manifested in the aggregate (civil rights, black na-
tionalism, etc.) but also in the interpersonal relationships, ac-
tions, and reactions between blacks and whites where taken
into account. When those "two lean cats," Baldwin and Mailer,
met in a French living room, it was precisely this power equa-
tion that was at work.
It is fascinating to read (in *Nobody Knows My Name*) in what
terms this power equation was manifested in Baldwin's imme-
diate reaction to that meeting: "And here we were, suddenly,
circling around each other. We liked each other at once, but
each was frightened that the other would pull rank. He could
have pulled rank on me because he was more famous and *had
more money* and also *because he was white;* but I could have pulled

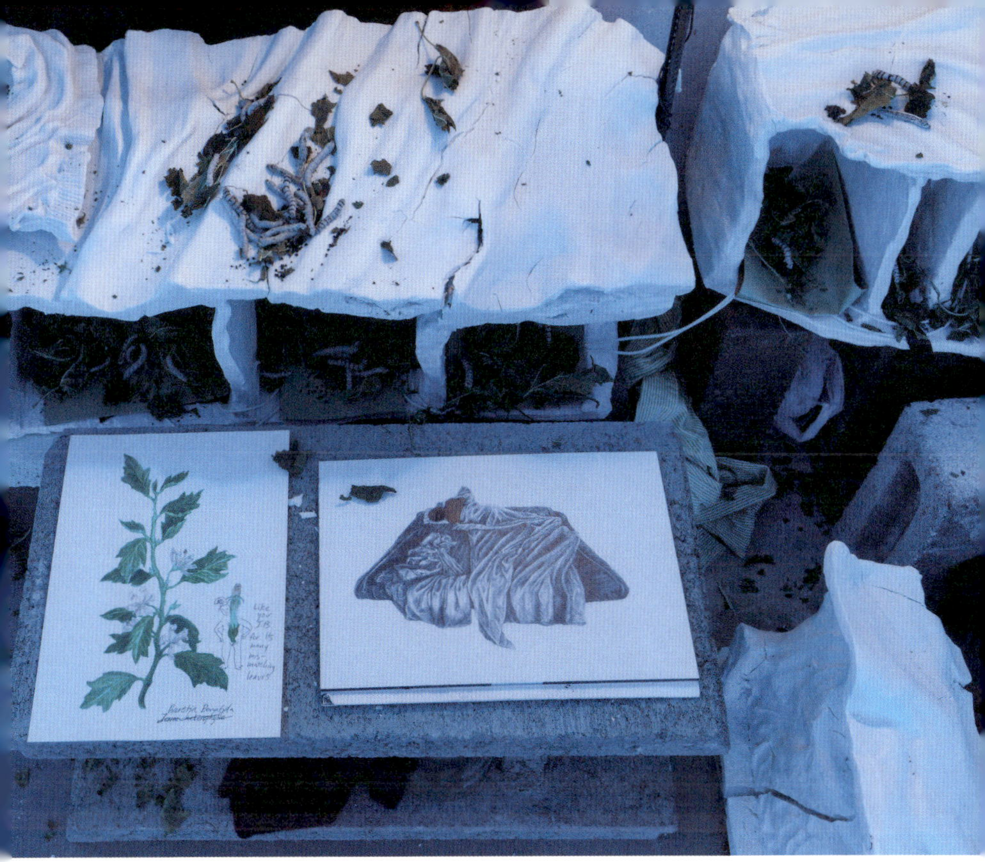

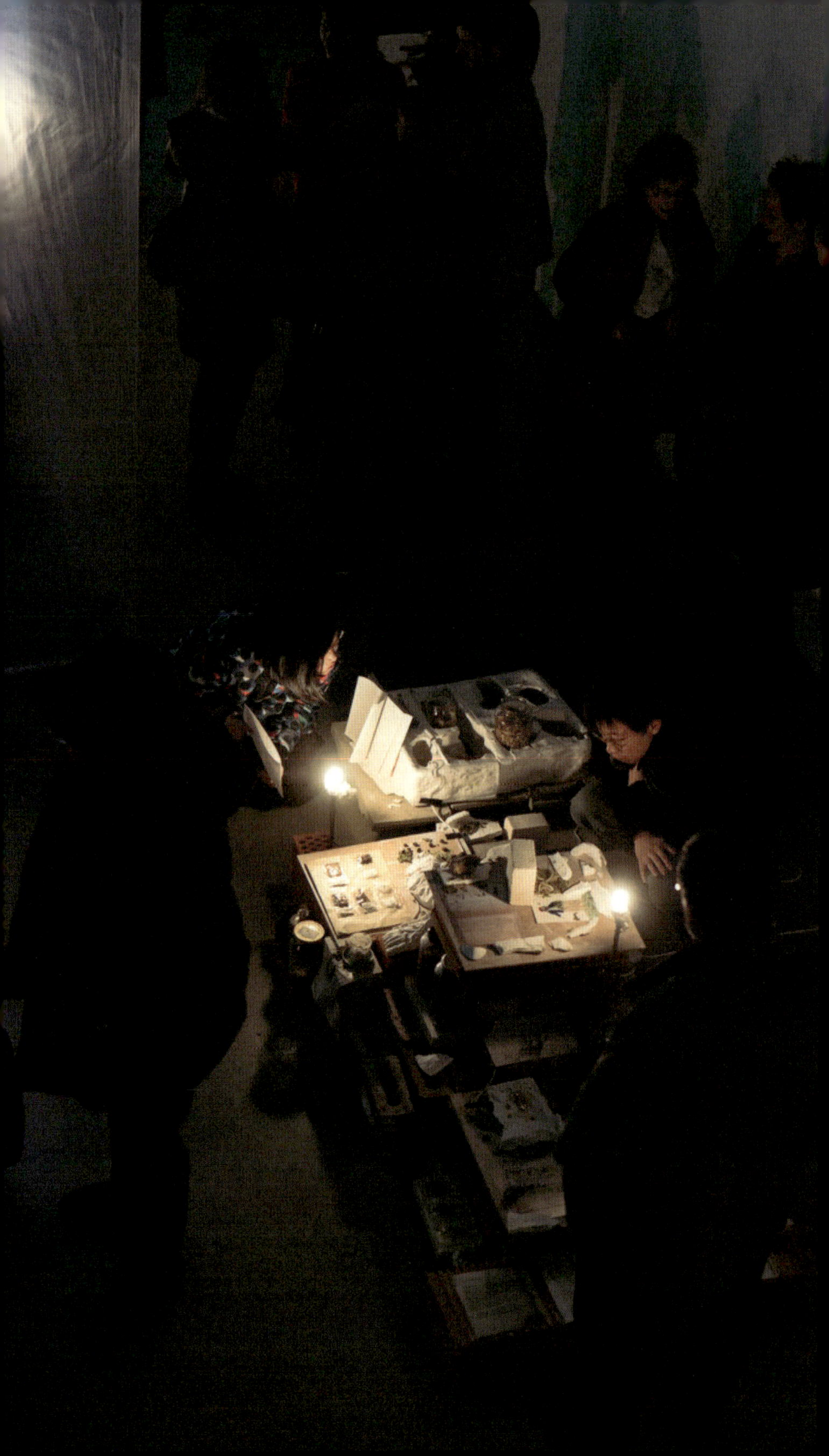

A (POST)-APOCALYPTIC CALL TO KNOWLEDGE AND ACTION

MEL Y. CHEN
AND
JIH-FEI CHENG

Incandescent light pours through the glass partitions of the Hammer Museum in Los Angeles. Washes of pink and purple highlight the artifice of the exhibition's enclosure. Entering the installation *La Charada China* (2018)[1] by artist Candice Lin, one finds at the center of the display a mound of dirt shaped into an altar, rectangular and coffin-like in form. The rough impression of a human body lies at its center (fig. 1). Voices and sounds narrating histories of agricultural labor emerge from a video installation positioned above. Photographs, drawings, notes, and personal effects that possibly belonged to laborers are nestled before the altar. Subterranean tubes emit a slight mist that seeps through the dirt, lending it a darkened, damp tinge.

This environment condenses the histories of nineteenth-century enslaved and indentured African, Indigenous, and Asian laborers across the Americas—and particularly in Cuba—with our present conditions of ecological disaster and labor exploitation. In both its title—which translates as "The Chinese Charade"—and its forms, the installation evokes the syncretic cultures and practices of play that sustained the racialized bodies forced to work on colonial plantations under duress. The "charade" in question is a Cuban-Chinese game that involved the pooling and circulation of capital; the winners of each round applied their earnings to their own needs. The stories *La Charada China* summons don't end with this past.

URGENCY, ACTION, AND THE (RE)CALL TO KNOWLEDGE

Engaging Lin's art means especially that we must pause and carefully consider how she combines theory and practice—praxis—to presence intertwined colonial histories. As feminists engaged in cultural studies, transnational queer theory, science and disability studies, and critical race studies, we are drawn to the suggestion, found amid Lin's installations, that ecological devastation is bound up with histories and hierarchies of settlement, race, gender, sexuality, ability, and species. The dismantling of ecologies is not simply about a human orientation toward disaster; rather, it marks a persistence of investment in

1. . . . . . This work was exhibited from June to September 2018 at the Hammer Museum as part of *Made in L.A. 2018*. A second iteration, presented at the 11th Taipei Biennial, was on view at the time of this writing.

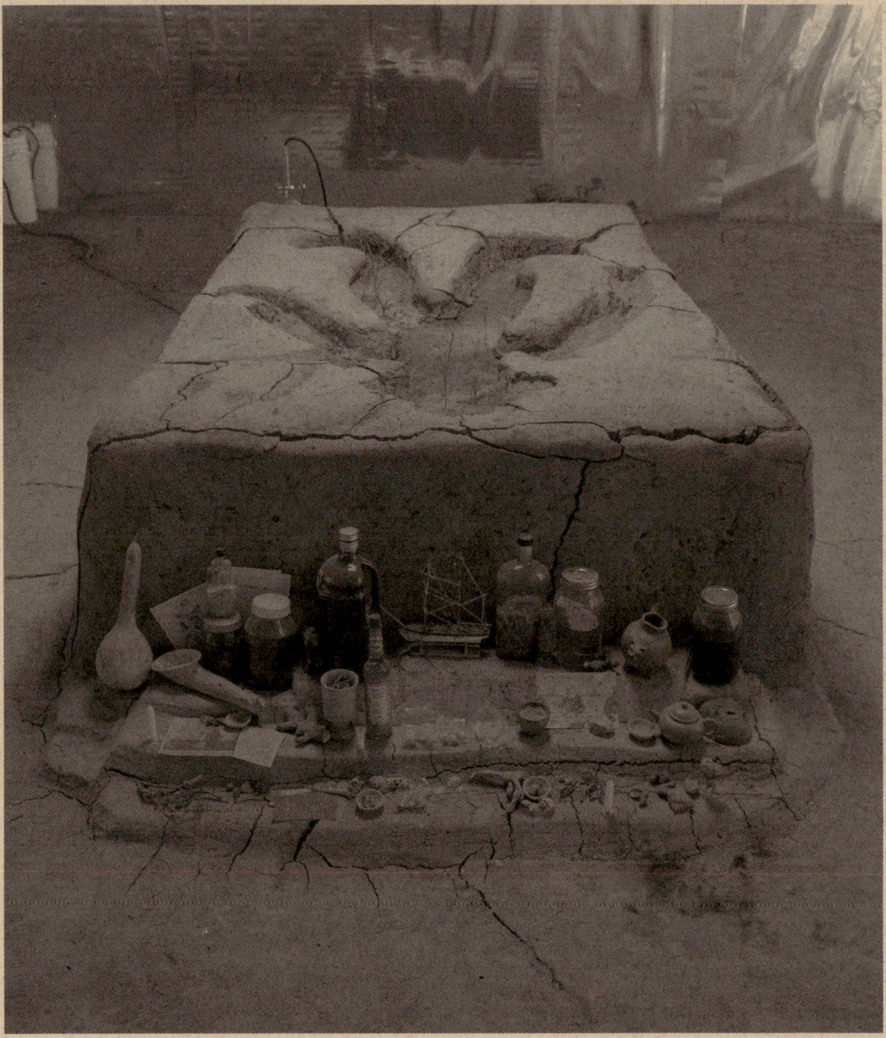

Fig. 1
La Charada China, 2018. Installation view of Made in L.A. 2018, Hammer Museum at the University of California, Los Angeles

resource and labor extraction across a variety of living and non-living entities. Lin's works press us to consider how our bodies and consciousness nurture, resist, or exploit ecologies that refuse containment and easy extraction. Thus, when we think about the primarily scientific focus on climate change today, we must face how "calls to action" can lead us up the wrong tree—or narrow our focus to just one tree in an ever-diminishing forest. By extension, we argue that to cling to disciplinary dogmas and scientific truths is too often to concede to the ideological transformations underway. Lin's work leads us not to a clearing but rather to a dense thicket of thinking, being, and action. We engage Lin's art as a recall to augmented, decolonial knowledge within and next to an augmented, decentered (in)humanism.[2]

But as genuine environmental and political crises abound worldwide, one wonders: Is it too late? There are ample declarations of "too late" in "this time of the Anthropocene," though this sentiment is scarce within academic humanist thought. While literary theory is rife with treatments of death, reflections on climate-related death are much less common. Too late, of course, begs the question of precisely what or whom it is too late for. Too late for sheer, bare life? For thriving? For untrammeled capitalism? For grassroots self-determination? For reversing the increasing disregulation and destruction of climate that promotes the collective exhaustion of human beings and humanness? For most of the above it would in fact be indulgently fatalistic to declare it too late, even if this may soon be technically true. We feel therefore that we need to be specific about both our pessimism and our determination. It is not necessarily ignorant to focus on vitality and survival, a "serious game" that *La Charada China* dramatizes. Such serious games represent the beauty and importance of becoming together, even if that becoming has an injurious past and present and a more precarious future—these acts are necessary methods and modes of living. What would it mean to spiritually align academic practice with micro modes of thriving such as this, even as we pursue longue durée modes of becoming-gone as a macro species?

2. . . . . . Dana Luciano and Mel Y. Chen, "Introduction: Has the Queer Ever Been Human?" *GLQ: A Journal of Lesbian and Gay Studies* 21, nos. 2–3 (June 2015): 183–207.

If we critically examine the historical chain of events and what has transpired, then we are already living in post-apocalyptic[3] times, even as things seem to grow worse. The institutionalized knowledge frameworks that we have grown familiar with must thus be signposted accordingly. What does it mean to comprehend ecological disaster not as a portent of the future but instead as part of a historicized present filled with palimpsestic conditions of violence, exploitation, and erasure? If the piling-up of colonial injuries Lin points to is so deeply woven into the present, perhaps to the point where ecologies of capitalism overwhelm (absent) the human, and if the identities of things in these ecologies (and the names we might use for them) stretch beyond our usual ken, then the common refrain (voiced, increasingly, in despair) becomes what is to be done? Mirroring this, our academic coconspirators also ask (likewise in despair): What (the heck) are we doing? At the time of this writing, in fact, the Trump administration is moving to un-recognize climate science, gender diversity, and indeed gender science.[4] Yet materialities organic and inorganic press forward polymorphically—these are the very energies, flows, and integrities that artists such as Lin (particularly in her other works) track. How might we reckon with what are opposing recognitions, or at least moves to recognize or dis-recognize? Is there a way to do this without reasserting master accounts? Or is it actually time to develop stark, universalistic master accounts? All such questions have bearing on method, as each of us is in a position to engage in activities we call "work," particularly "research" and "pedagogy." How we have chosen to conceptualize this work in relation to time yields something like a post-apocalyptic methodological approach—one that ideally can accommodate the apocalypses of the past and also anticipate those to come. Some might say this is too high a bar. But perhaps a game like the one Lin shows does exactly that, through cycles of short-lived turns. If theory attends to macro species considerations, living attaches more tightly to the temporalities of the small scale, wherein apocalypse finds actual expression and can be met by contravening forces.

3. . . . . . See Michelle Murphy, *Seizing the Means of Reproduction: Entanglements of Feminism, Health, and Technoscience* (Durham, NC: Duke University Press, 2012); Christina Sharpe, *In the Wake: On Blackness and Being* (Durham, NC: Duke University Press, 2016); Anna Lowenhaupt Tsing, *The Mushroom at the End of the World: On the Possibility of Life in Capitalist Ruins* (Princeton, NJ: Princeton University Press, 2017).

What is the (in)humanistic method at this juncture? Can it be found in the idea that the work of a given discipline proceeds under its own integrity (which isn't true), or in the idea that the reality to which a set of theories refers has outpaced theory altogether? In a 2009 essay called "The Climate of History: Four Theses," Dipesh Chakrabarty described the inadequacy of existing apprehensions of history within the discipline itself. The latter depends on the discourse of globalization, which in turn developed in parallel with climate change studies, and history was ill prepared for the planetary, temporal, and social cuts of climate change. More generally, then, how do we already move within and across, through and with, the materials we're working with given the times? Quite to the contrary of precision, we could make a case here for conceptual nondistinction, or a retreat from certainties that we identify as operating deviously to further the destructions that capitalism and colonialism have made commonsense or habitual. For these, the queer, anticolonial, critical race, feminist methods of analysis we find in our work remain true. In these modes, what might look from the outside like categorical equivocation (or, indeed, game playing) are actually forms of productive suspension in the name of massive truth-seeking.

OCCUPATIONS OF TIME: REFUSING FASCIST TEMPORALITIES

Working amid multiple social, political, economic, and environmental crises, we are prompted to think of fascism as a historical break from democracy, a diversion from progress. Yet what is happening right now across governments and in our interconnected environments is that the crises that form liberal democracies are being revealed as always in concert with fascisms.[5] The time of "work," its necessity, and the limited capacity some of us have to

4. . . . . . As of this writing, the Trump administration has withdrawn the United States' participation from the Paris Agreement, a plan spearheaded by the United Nations to address climate change. It is also attempting to work with the U.S. Department of Health and Human Services to dismantle protections for intersex, trans, non-binary gender, and gender nonconforming peoples. Meanwhile, the Trump administration has declared that "gender" is not based upon science and that therefore all references to gender should be based upon genitalia at birth.

5. . . . . . The sweep of fascism in the face of growing insecurity and ecological instability demonstrates how globalized capitalism simultaneously induces and seizes upon environmental crises. What we are witnessing now is a "turn away from democracy, towards authoritarianism, in a great thunderous wave . . . [that has] rippled outward from . . . America, like a supersonic tsunami, crossing Europe, reaching Asia's shores, crashing south into Brazil, cresting far away in Australia." See Umair Haque, "Why Catastrophic Climate Change is Probably Inevitable Now: How Capitalism Torched the Planet by Imploding Into Fascism," *Eudaimonia*, October 10, 2018, https://eand.co/how-capitalism-torched-the-planet-and-left-it-a-smoking-fascist-greenhouse-fe687e99f070.

sell our labor preoccupy us. We are living in what Walter Benjamin has described as a "state of distraction," where the value of art, and of life itself, rests in its verisimilitude or proximity to an imagined original or ideal. Work occupies our notions of time and what is possible. It guides our attention away from class elitism, resource privatization, and the growing forms of authoritarianism and militarism that choke life—while also feeding their proliferation.

La Charada China foregrounds the intellectual and creative work of the artist. This praxis is cast through the historical labor of racialized bodies and conjures present-day Los Angeles as a site whose urban sprawl cannot be cordoned off from histories of Native dispossession, African enslavement, and Asian indentured servitude and national exclusion. If Los Angeles is "home" to Euro-American empire, its inhabitants continue to challenge gentrification and the racial profiling of Black and Latinx peoples. La Charada China reminds us that the droughts, earthquakes, and massive fires experienced by the city and its inhabitants are a combined result of forms of settler colonialism and environmental racism—including land speculation, resource hoarding, the dismantling of public services, and the increasing reliance on private and expensive forms of insurance.

LOSING DISCRETENESS

Discreteness of phenomena and categorical boundaries, along with analytic precision, are presumed to be desirable within scientific and academic work. One example found in both meta-discourses is taxonomy. However, we find that discreteness can function as a troubled habit of analytic conservatism that, if attached to a worldscape whose segregations came about through colonial imprints, cannot function as a "building block" for the production of revolutionary or reimaginative knowledge. This is what so many interdisciplinary scholars of gender and sexuality, indigeneity, and race have experienced so deeply.

Let us now consider La Charada China as a micro mode of thriving, one that requires a productive traffic, such that the clear identity (or extractability) of any of them is haunted, blocked, or foreclosed.

Lin's work unglues the structural and mundane forms

of racist, misogynistic, and heteropatriarchal violence: buried in the mixture of red clay, cement, and animal excrement that she brought with her from the Dominican Republic are the seeds of poppies, sugarcane, and tropical plants. These seeds evoke the entwined histories of Euro-American colonization across the Atlantic and Pacific, including the British opium trade in China, Native dispossession, and African enslavement across the Americas—pasts that refuse burial. Forced by these materials to reckon with various persistent "pests"—plants, insects, mold, and more—the Hammer Museum fumigated the exhibition to prevent the gallery space from being overtaken.

The figurations within *La Charada China* trace the "global trade routes" that pave today's continual forced removals of Native peoples; the carceral geographies that mitigate/circumscribe Black social, economic, and political mobilities; and the forced migrations of non-white bodies for the purposes of low- and no-wage labor. This work demonstrates how the forms of ongoing colonial extraction nevertheless give way to ecologies of resistance and contamination that force social movements to recognize the integral involvements of interspecies and transspecies, as well as of material and non-material worlds.

The seeds, whose interactions within the "white box" environment of the museum gallery are unpredictable, manifest ecologies of trauma and resistance. Their growth forces the recognition that survival entails losing discreteness, not by leveling differences but—as intersectional analyses reveal—by acknowledging our enmeshment through micro modes of thriving during post-apocalyptic times.

With our attention turned toward the scale of the "micro" in our respective work, we find that we, and our work, are already entangled with Lin.

SLOWNESS AND AGITATION

Whether understood as drugs or poisons or as means of comfort or control, micro substances like opium were used to animate and temporalize disabled-racialized difference in radically diverse ways. One example Chen has drawn upon in their work is the London clinic of John Langdon

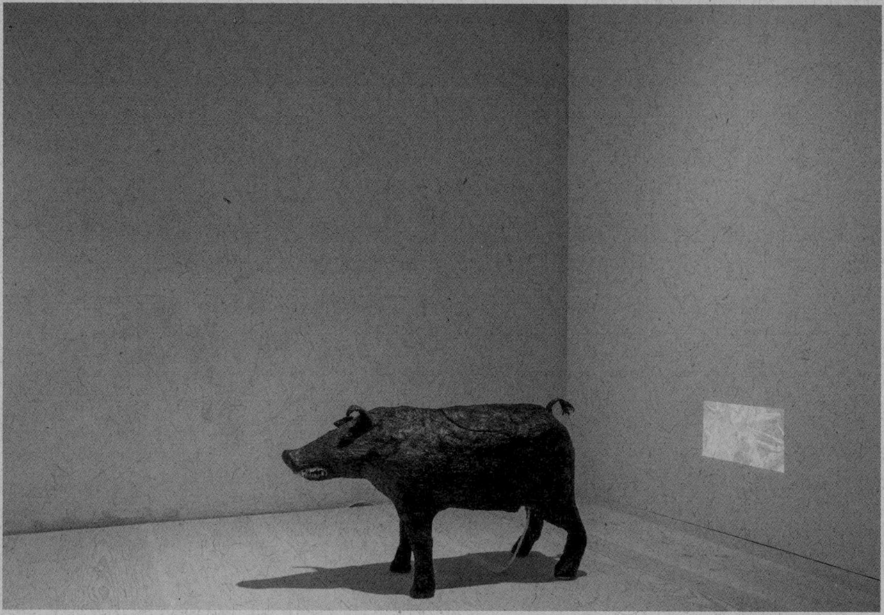

Fig. 2
Bacium Sub Cauda (kiss under the tail), 2012. Installation view of Politics of Food at Delfina Foundation, London, 2014

Down, who was known for his assertion of "mongoloid idiocy" as a racial form of developmental delay, a claim that substantiates both slowness and race with each other's materialities. (Opium, furthermore, played a critical role in both clinical and diagnostic methods.) In a similar mode, agitation animates as a ghostly political form of embodied being, coded as racialized disability. If temporal-material registers like slowness and agitation are ways of describing the already contaminated movement between supposedly discrete things, there are also other ways of understanding the generation of incitement/movement. Entanglement thus seems like a more honest rendering than does a system based on the presumed stability of race or disability. Indeed, humans, nonhuman animals, microbiological organisms, and inanimate things have long been confounded via concepts of race that were grounded in the categorization and differentiation of living and non-living things.

(INTER/TRANS)SPECIES

In 2012 Lin exhibited *Bacium Sub Cauda (kiss under the tail)*, which "narrates the . . . slaughter of . . . Haitian pigs in 1982 [by] U.S. Agribusiness. Fearful that the African Swine Flu, detected in the Dominican Republic in 1978, would spread . . . the U.S. government . . . replac[ed them] with fragile U.S. pigs that required special pens and expensive feed that U.S. companies were paid to supply" (fig. 2).[6]

Cheng's research on the histories of white supremacy and Han Chinese ethnosupremacy has followed the importation of pigs, the industrialization of pig farming, and viral outbreaks across the Atlantic and the Pacific. Considering Lin's artistic praxis using the visual symbols of quotidian commerce, Cheng is able to draw forth a post-apocalyptic method for an augmented, decentered (in)humanism that analyzes together climate change and industrial waste.

In 2018 Hurricane Florence barreled toward the Carolinas where, on large factory farms, "cesspools" of hog waste collects in lagoons that are then sprayed like rain onto largely Black, Native, and Latinx communities that remain redlined and structurally vulnerable. North

6. . . . . . Candice Lin, "*It makes the patient see pictures*," unpublished artist statement in an email to Jih-Fei Cheng, September 6, 2018.

Carolina is the second largest producer of pork in the United States. The largest supplier, Smithfield, is now owned by the People's Republic of China.[7]

By heeding the colonial histories of pork production and consumption, we gain a clearer sense of how settler colonialism, slavery, agricultural industrialization, and climate change are part and parcel of today's environmental racism.

THE SCALAR FICTION

In chaos theory, the tale of the butterfly (a storied thought experiment among lay thinkers) models the general inadequacy of scale-based logics of consequentiality. Climate change has eclipsed the butterfly story, but both are "true." A recent book on Lyme disease echoes this parable of impact in the refrain but how could it be caused by just a little tick?[8] Global capitalism seems to operate at one scale but, of course, its mandate is that it must always scale up. So perhaps what we find in micro modes of thriving are the forms of mutuality, syncretism, and collective resistance to extractivism and scale itself. Thinking with reference to scale provides lyrical ways to move between the local, small, and intimate and on to the industrial and global. Despite, or perhaps precisely because of, the prevalence of capitalism, it is as important as ever to keep away from monolithic, monoscalar solutions that recapitulate capitalist scales of time, space, and progress.

We end with the question that we could also have begun with: what might a post-apocalyptic flow, born of love in the present, look like in (scholarly, creative, political interventional, and collaborative) form?

7. . . . . . See Erica Hellerstein and Ken Fine, "A million tons of feces and an unbearable stench: life near industrial pig farms," The Guardian, September 20, 2017, https://www.theguardian.com/us-news/2017/sep/20/north-carolina-hog-industry-pig-farms, and Doug Bock Clarke. "Why Is China Treating North Carolina Like the Developing World?" Rolling Stone, March 19, 2018, https://www.rollingstone.com/politics/politics-news/why-is-china-treating-north-carolina-like-the-developing-world-122892/.

8. . . . . . See Porochista Khakpour, Sick: A Memoir (New York: Harper Perennial, 2018).

REVA AND DAVID
LOGAN CENTER FOR THE ARTS
AT THE UNIVERSITY OF CHICAGO

PAGES 105–118
INSTALLATION VIEWS OF
A HARD WHITE BODY,
A POROUS SLIP

SEPTEMBER 14–OCTOBER 28, 2018

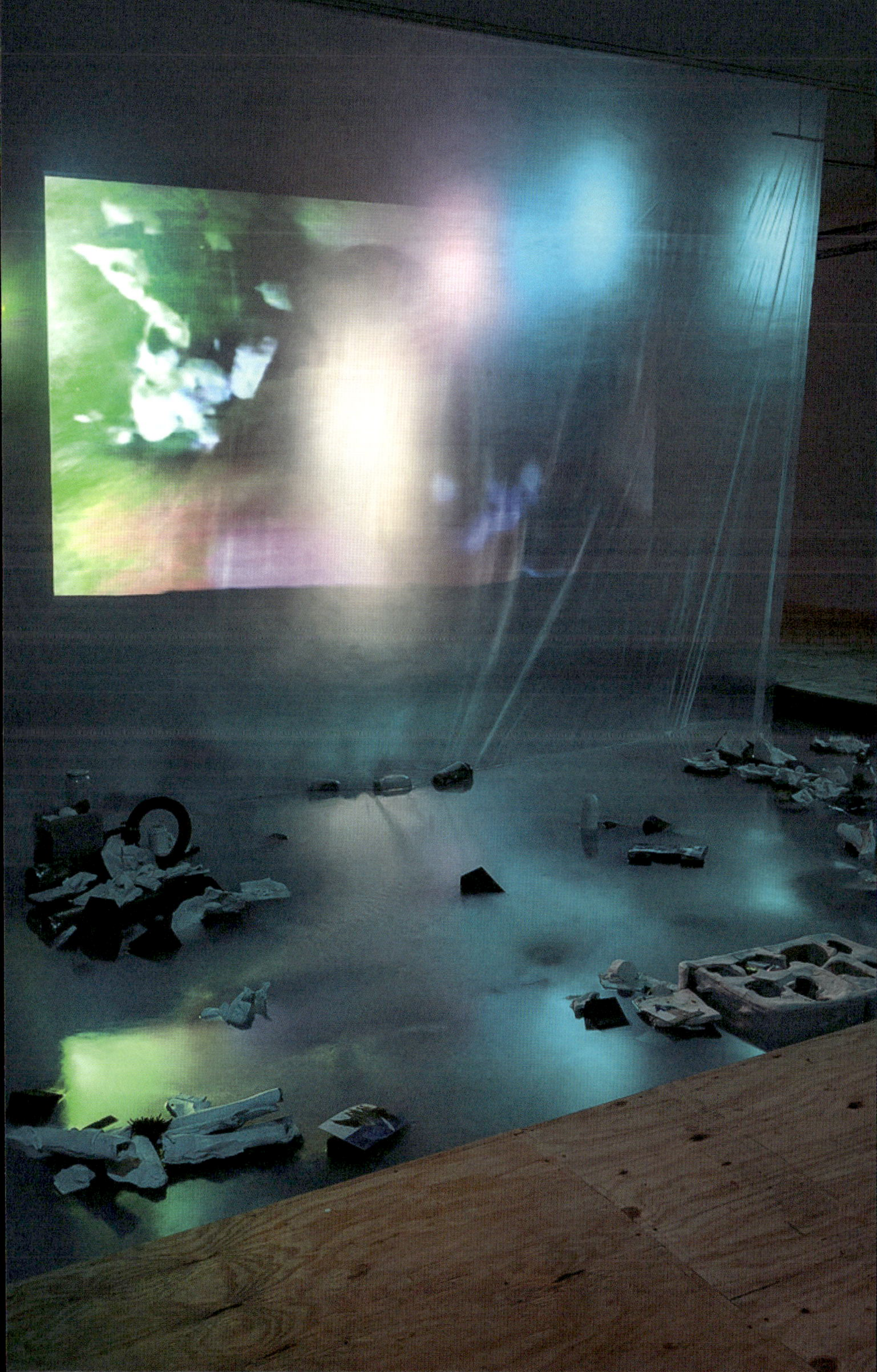

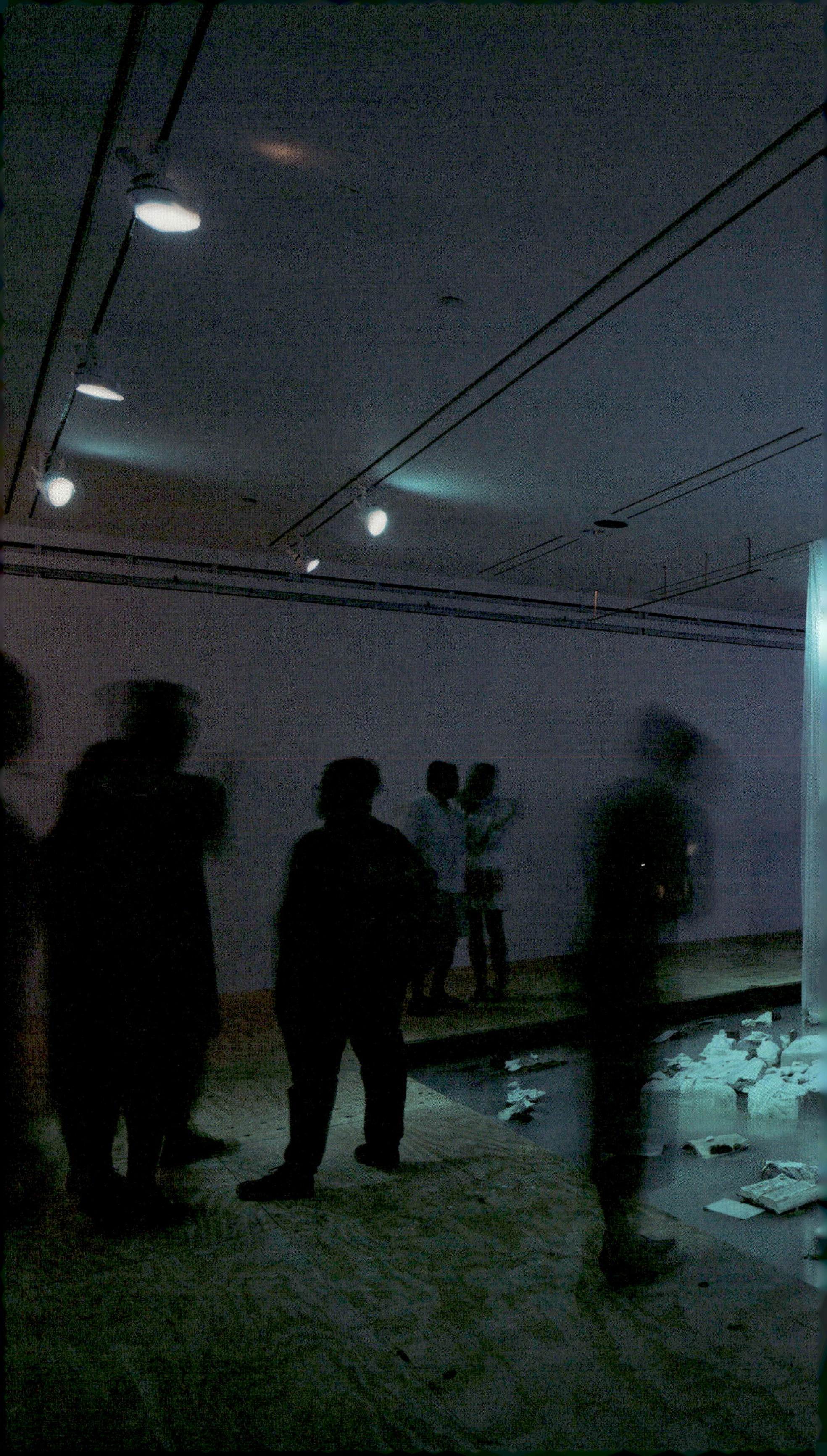

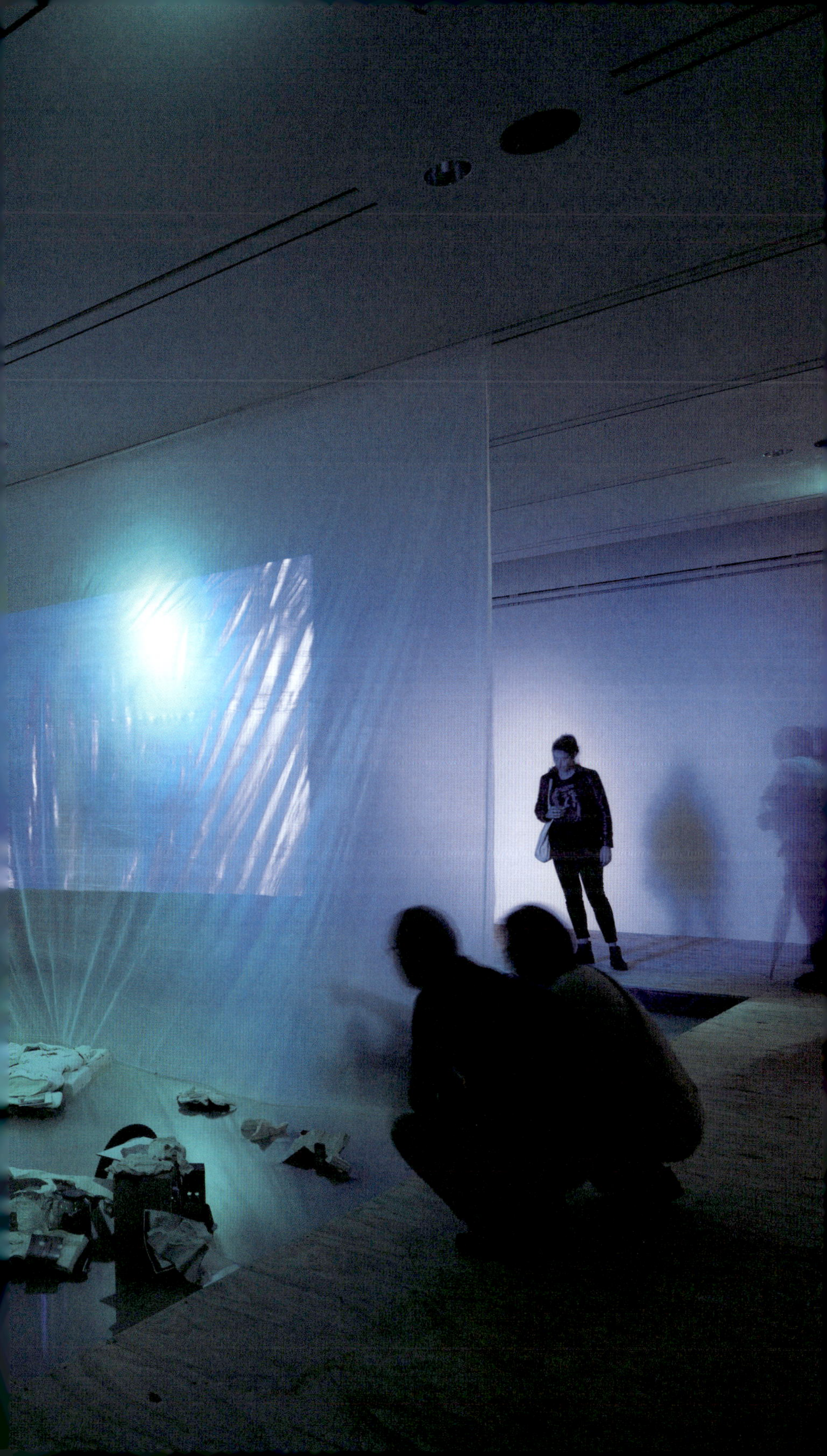

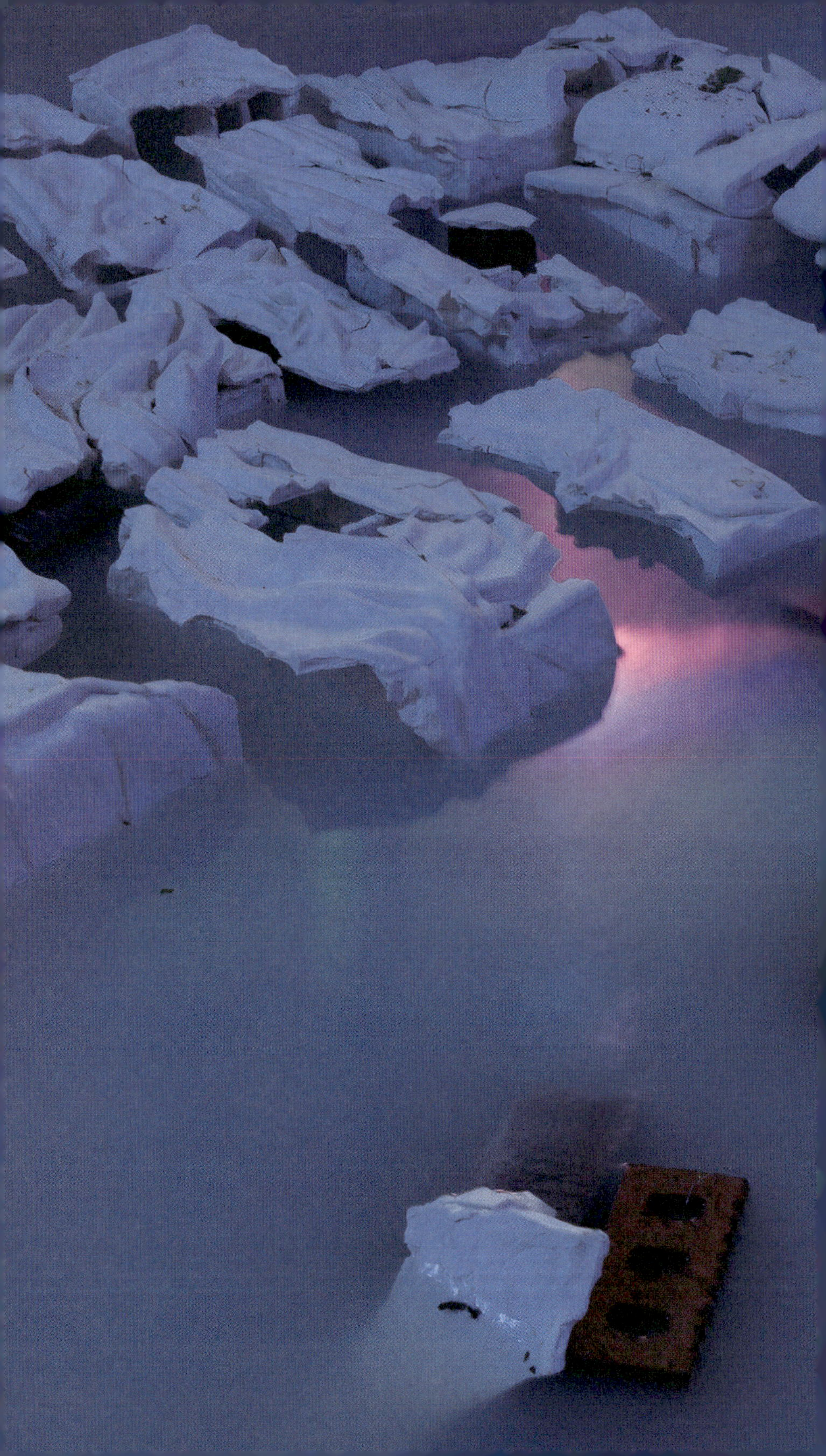

ICI ON NOIE LE
ALGERIENS

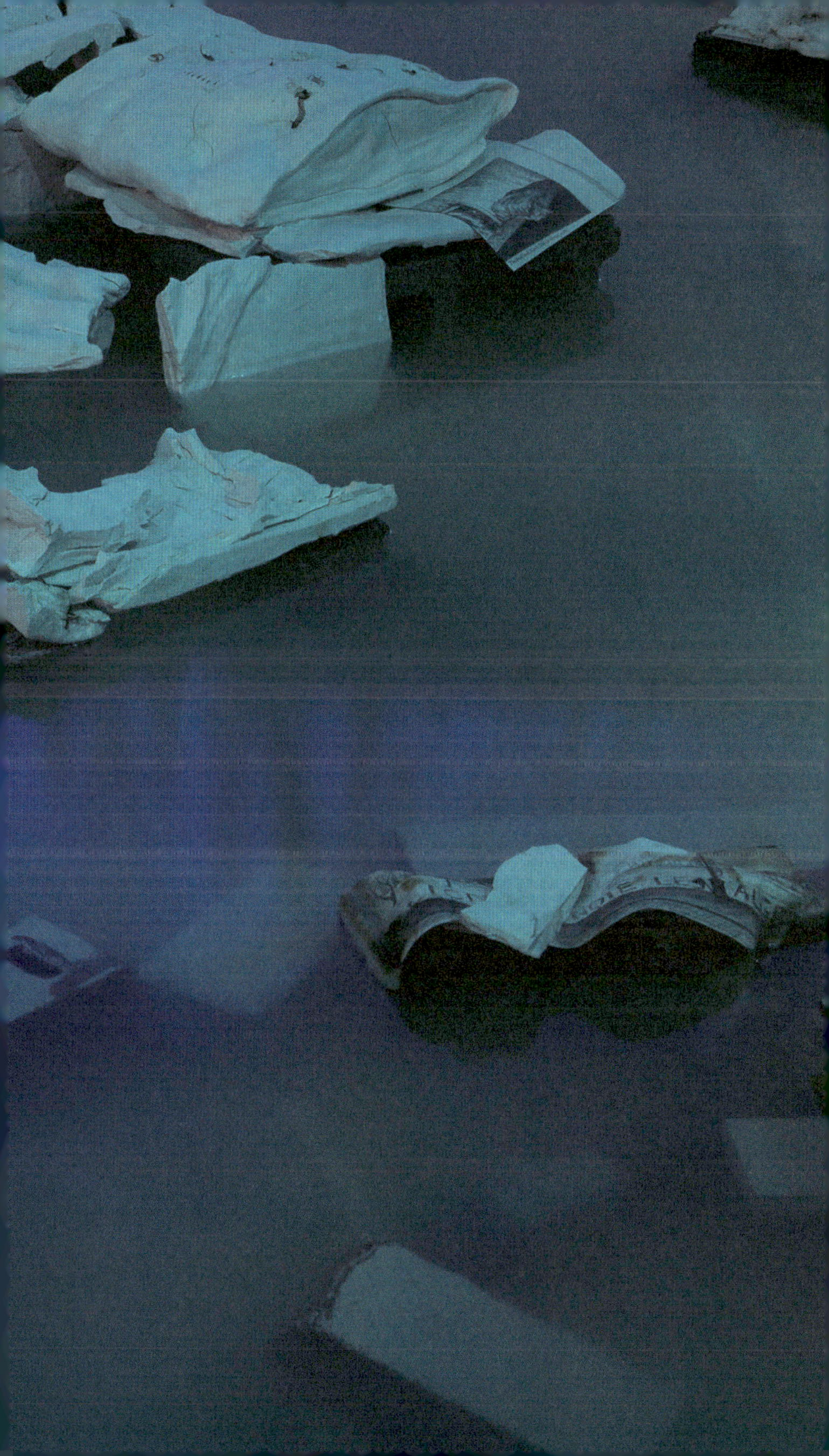

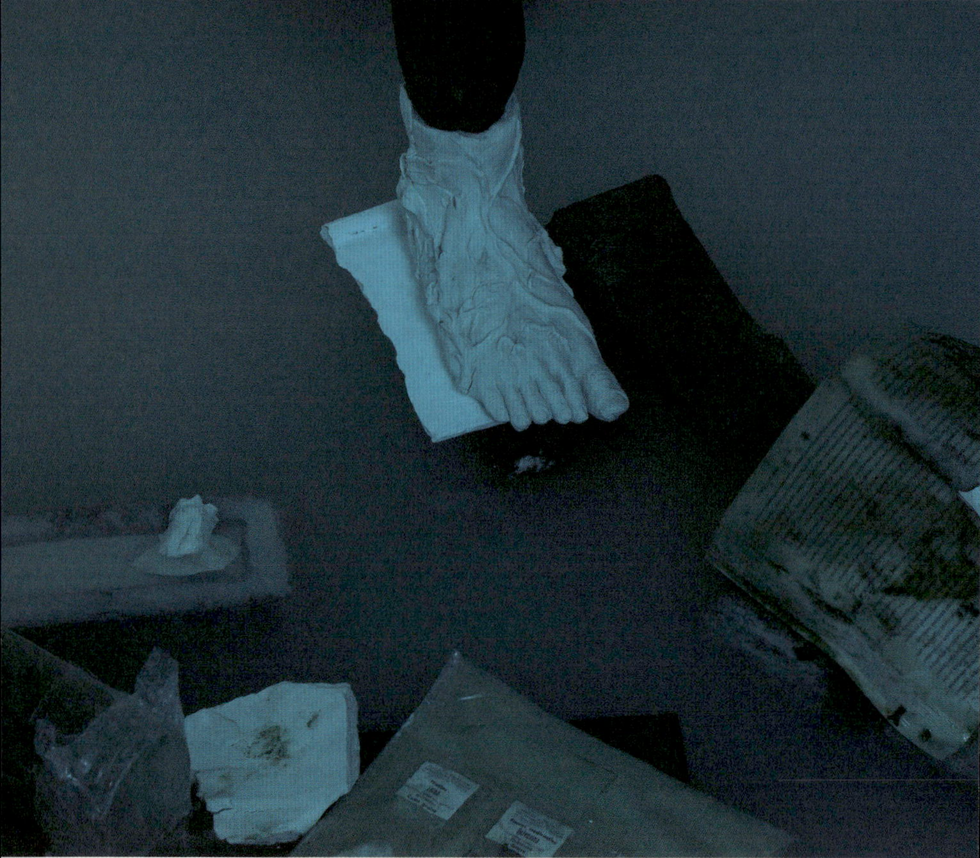

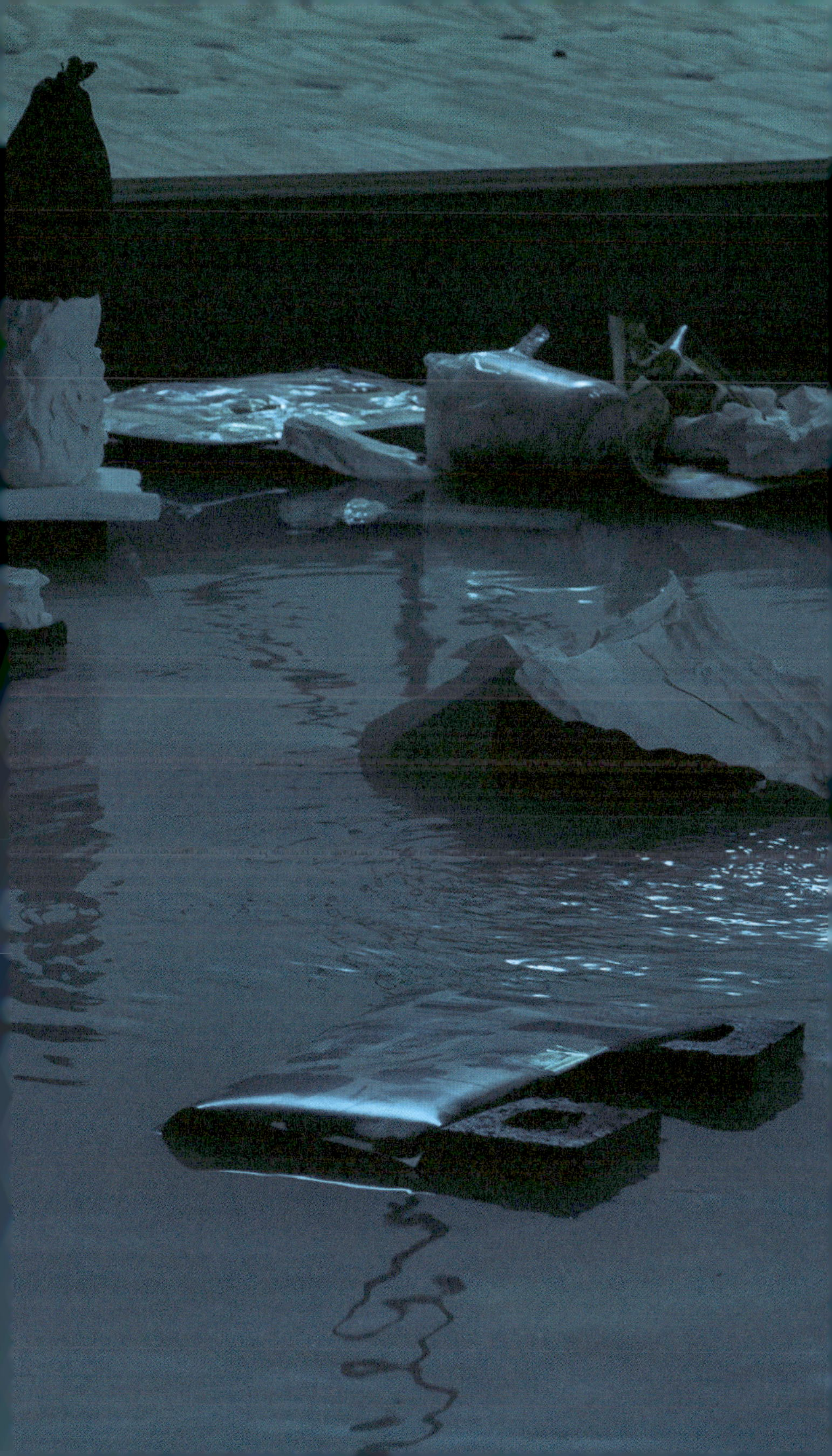

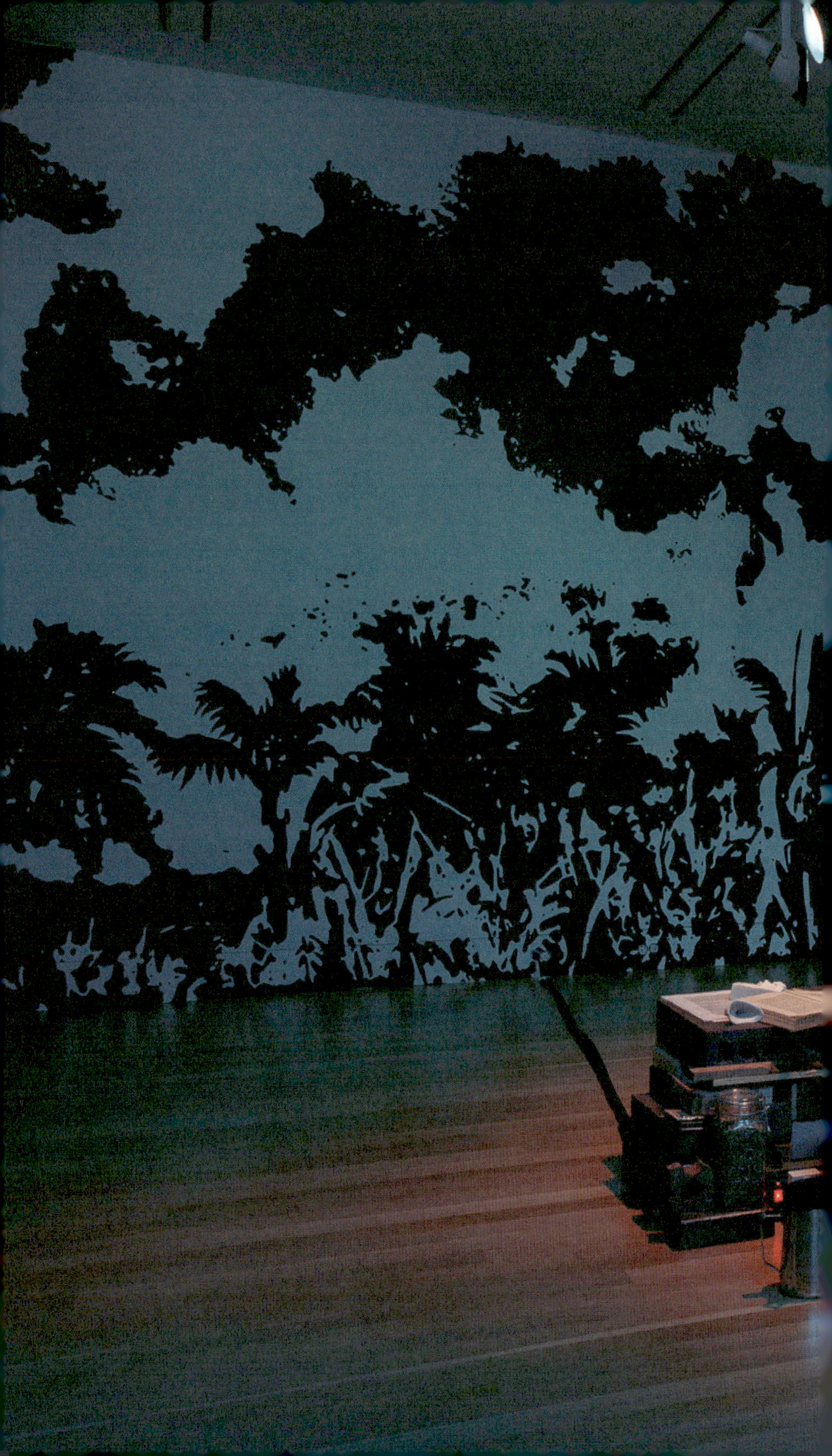

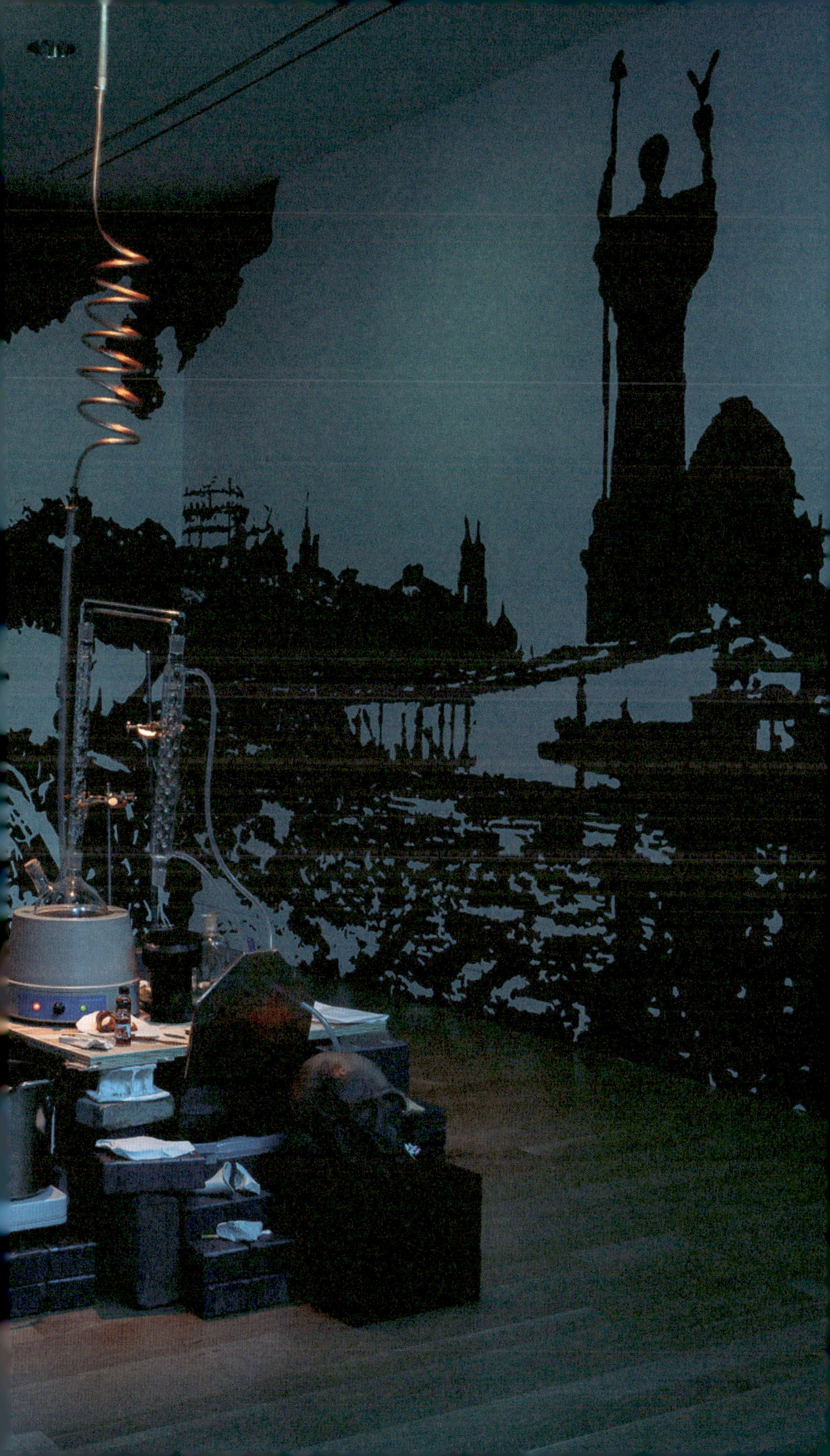

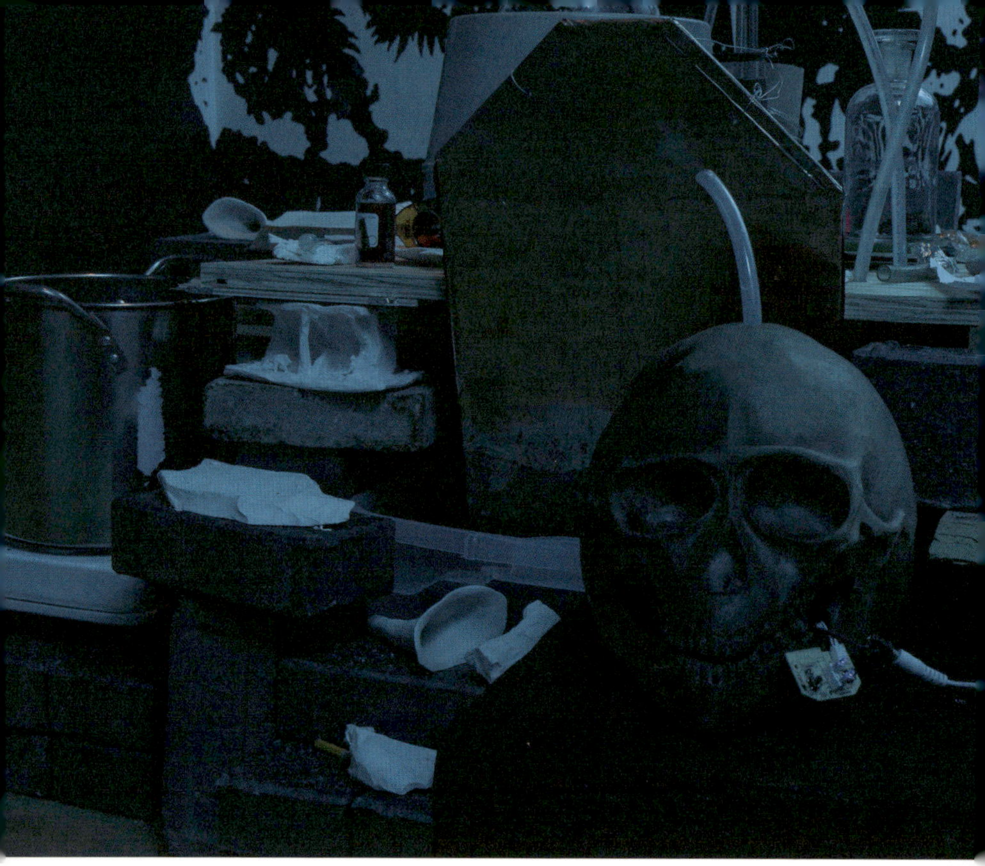

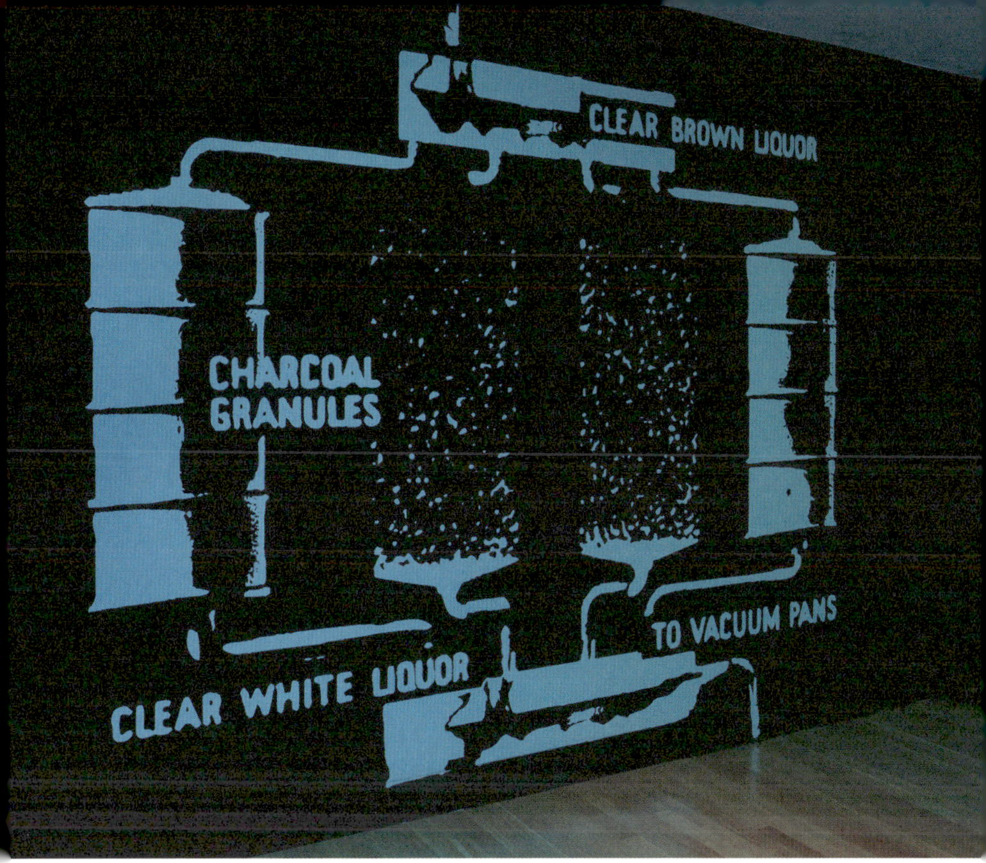
CLEAR BROWN LIQUOR
CHARCOAL
GRANULES
TO VACUUM PANS
CLEAR WHITE LIQUOR

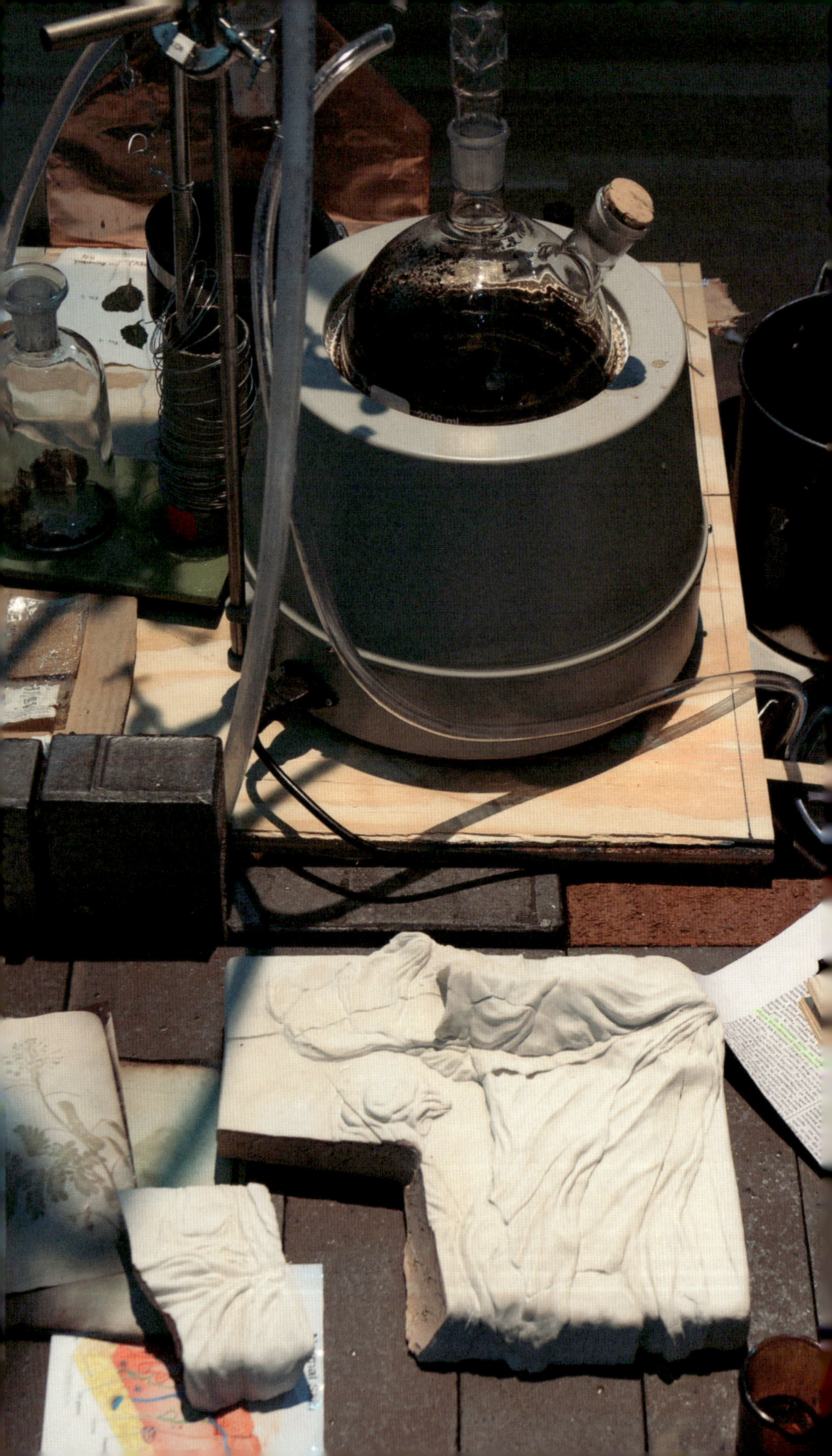

THE BELOVED

CANDICE LIN

Let me be your leg and carry you over mountains your gangrene cannot go.

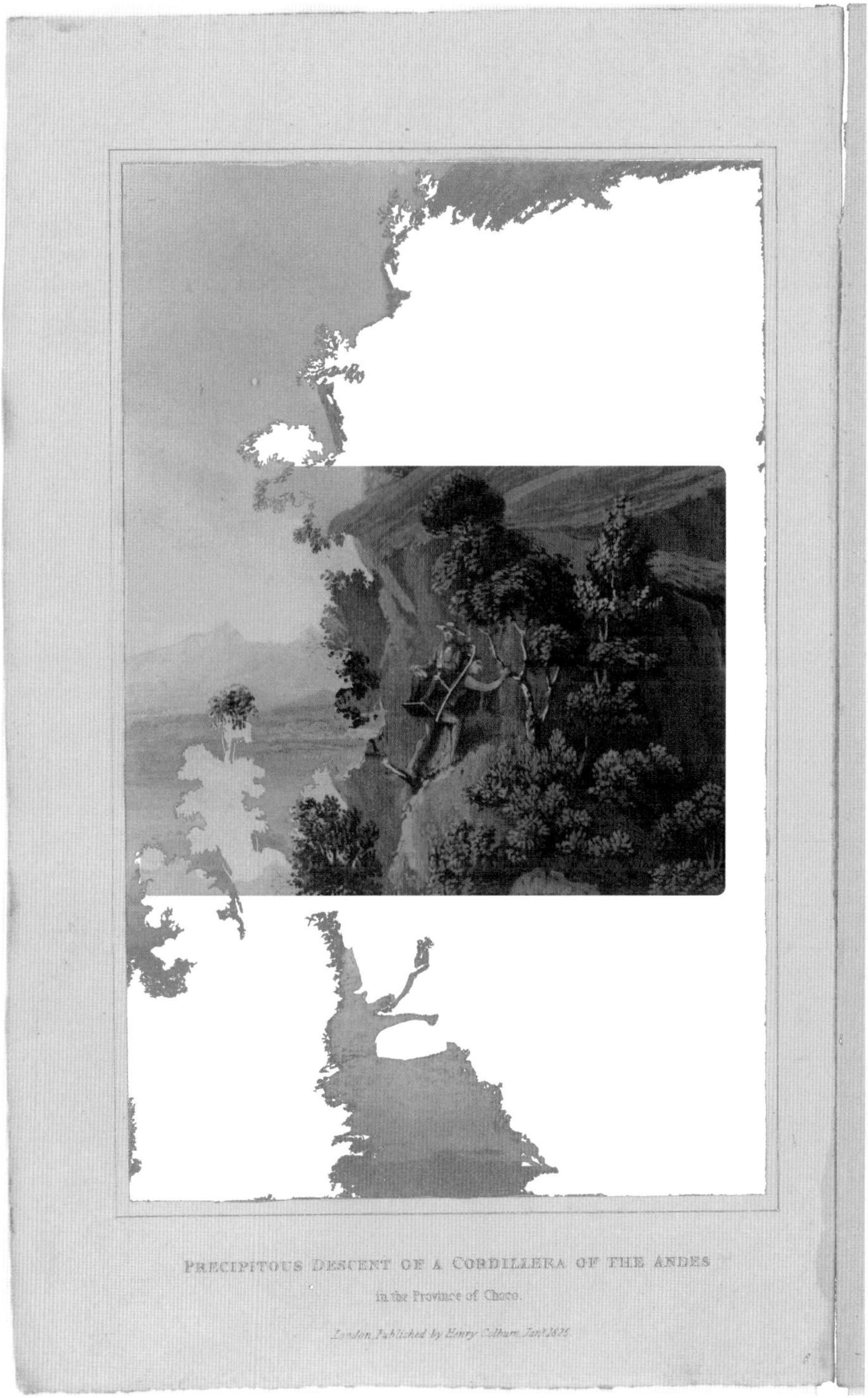

Let me describe to you the plants I found, the shape of their many leaves, how they flower in the winter and change sex when they begin to smell.

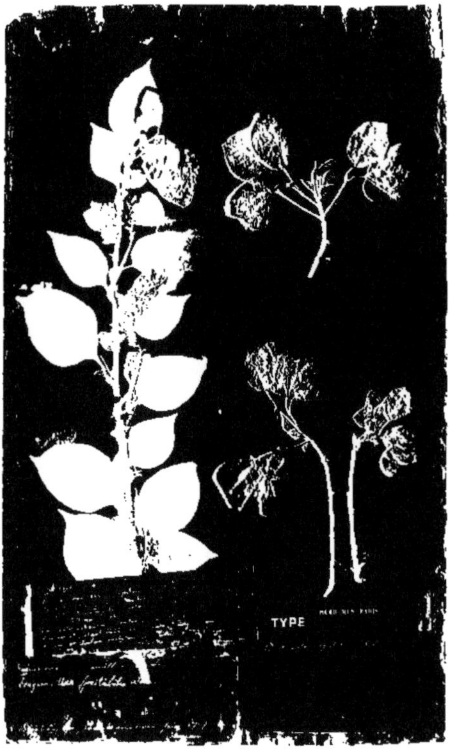

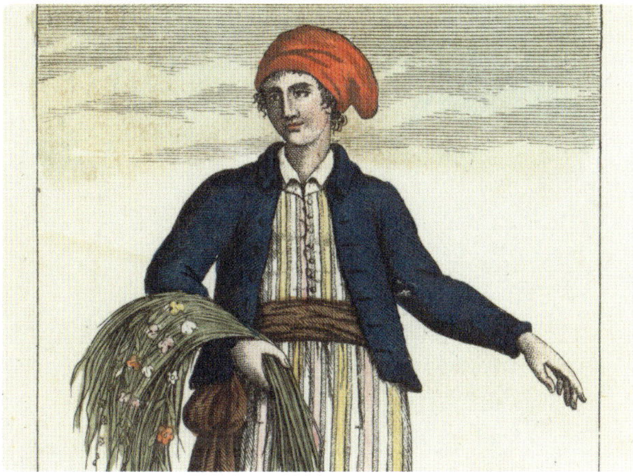

Jeanne Baret (July 27, 1740–August 5, 1807). The first woman to circumnavigate the globe, she did so cross-dressing as the male assistant to her employer and lover, botanist Philibert Commerson, on the French colonial expedition led by Louis-Antoine de Boungainville.

When your leg was so swollen it was the size of two, I cut the surface with a piece of glass and smeared a bean paste in the wound.

A list of plants thought to be written by Jeanne Baret, Found in the archives of Philibert Commerson.

Sometimes it helped and the pus came out. Temporarily, you felt better. You would sigh deeply and hold my head, murmuring to me, “oh my dearest, my beast of burden.”

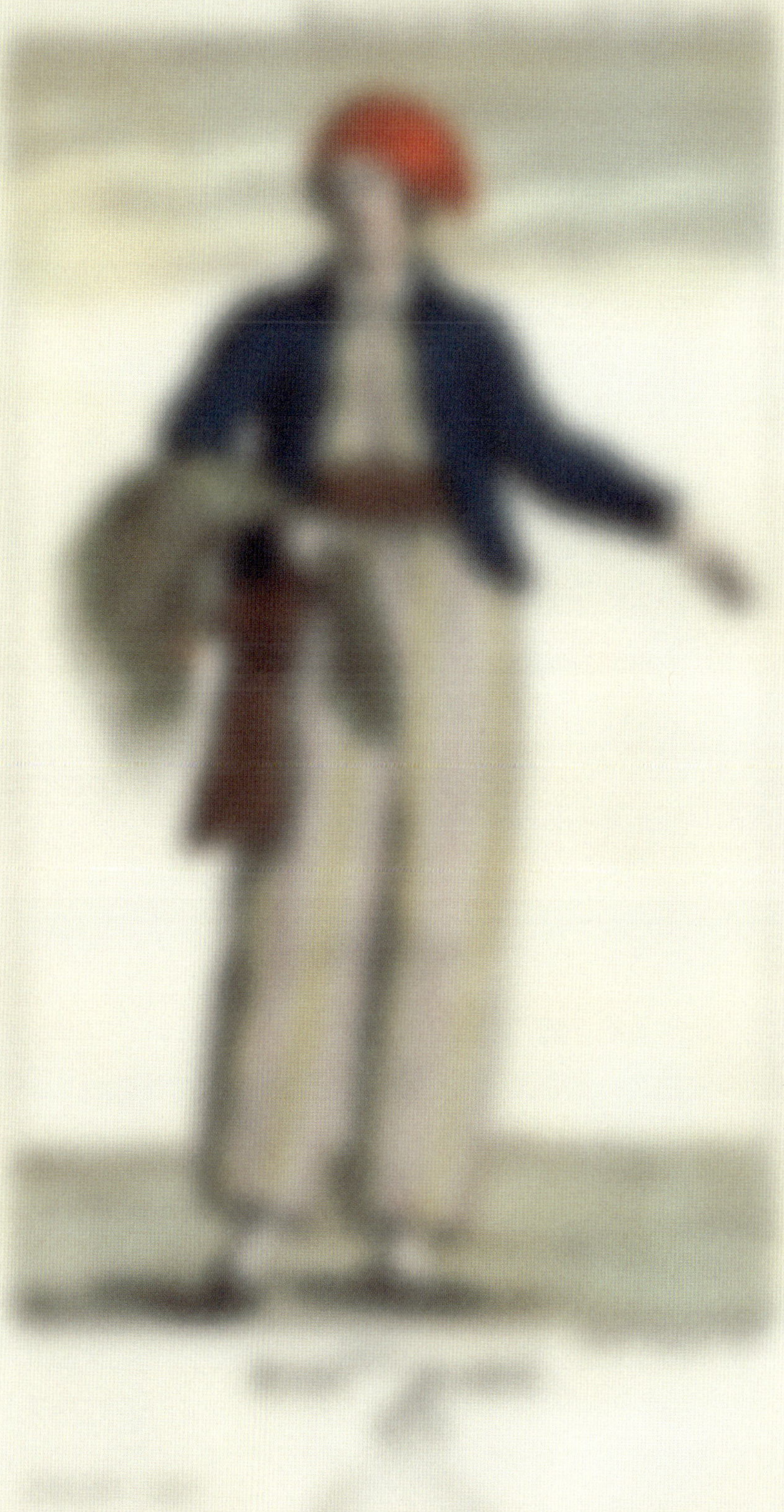

Other times, I could not find the right plant

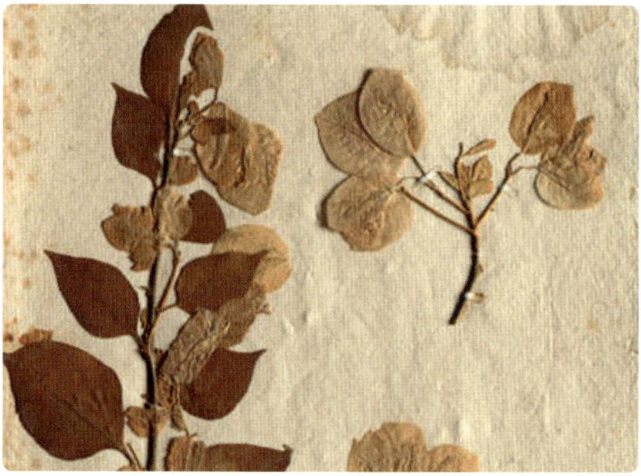

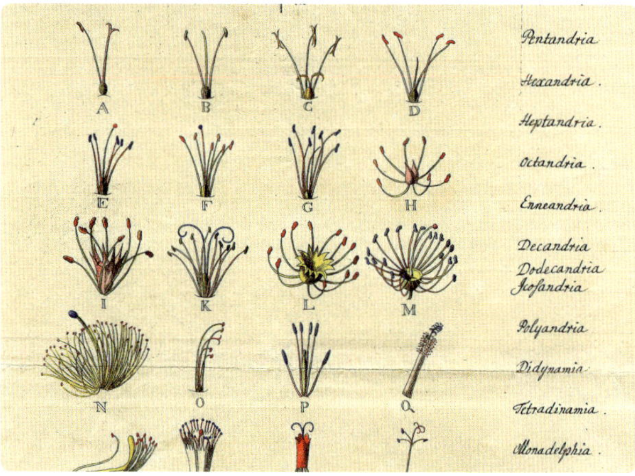

on these foreign islands,

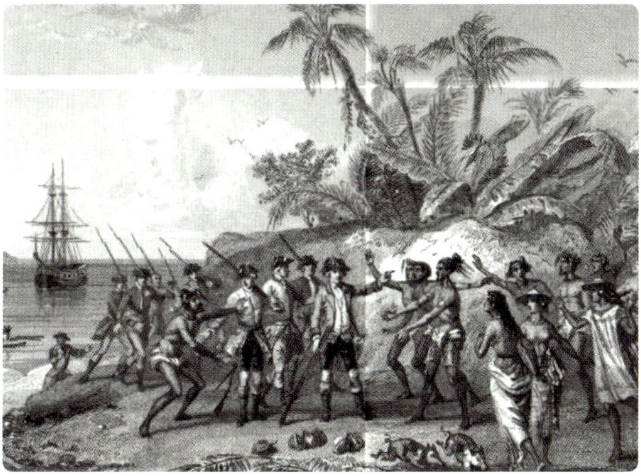

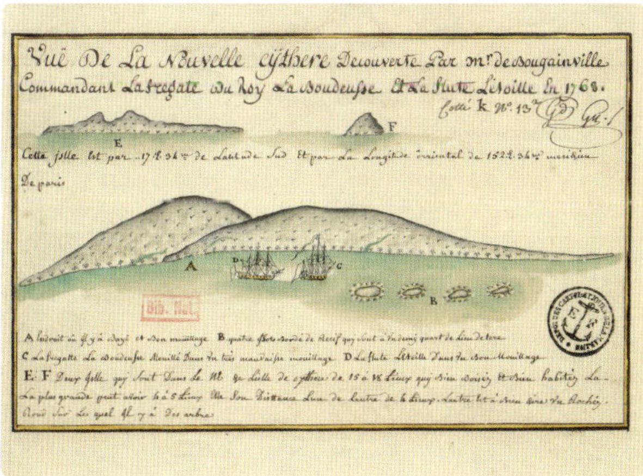

Depictions of Louis-Antoine de Bougainville's expedition arriving on Tahiti in 1768. Bougainville claimed Tahiti for the French and named it Nouvelle-Cythère.

and so I used the Law of Similars and found what appeared to be legumes. These caused poisonous welts and blisters and you cursed me for my peasant stupidity. But a foot cannot kick itself. We were bound.

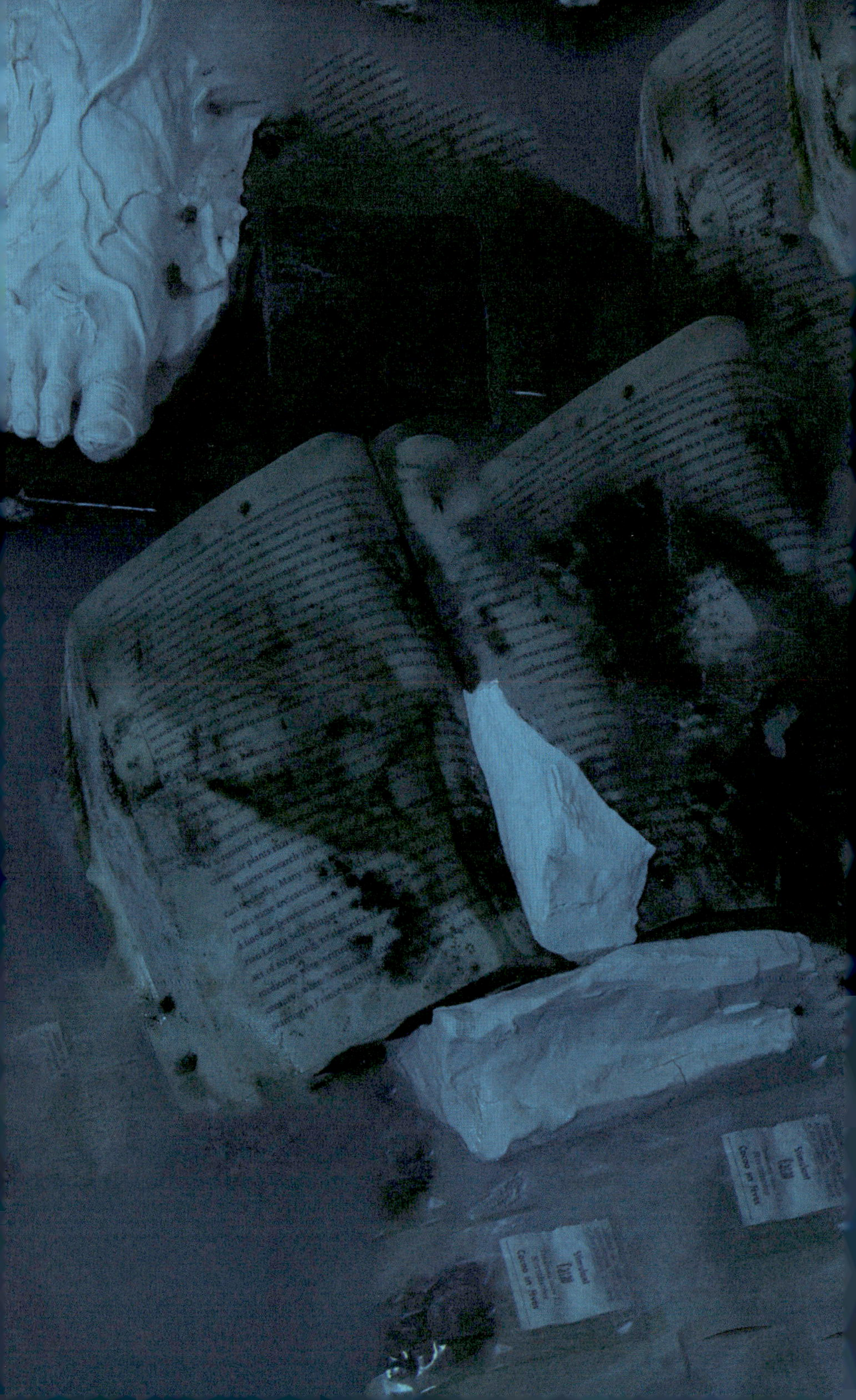

Before I was a peasant in the Loire Valley, I was a king, the Beloved, whose body was made of glass. All the courtiers would gather around with pillows stuffed with goose down, wrapping me in heavy woven blankets and rugs, protecting my fragility. The doctor said this was sickness. But he knew nothing of the plants that could be eaten to restore my animal flesh.

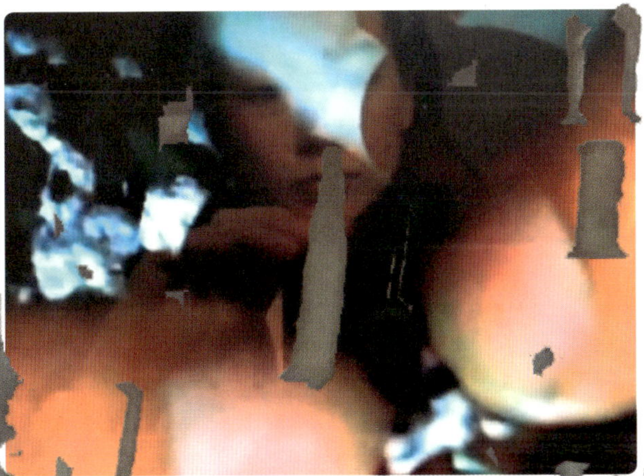

So he said, wrap her carefully and bring her to parties. And to parties we went, where they sang with bright musicality and moved their hips. They dressed us to look like wild men in textures of linen, moss, and pitch. Then they burned us, and I remembered how it felt to be made of flesh.

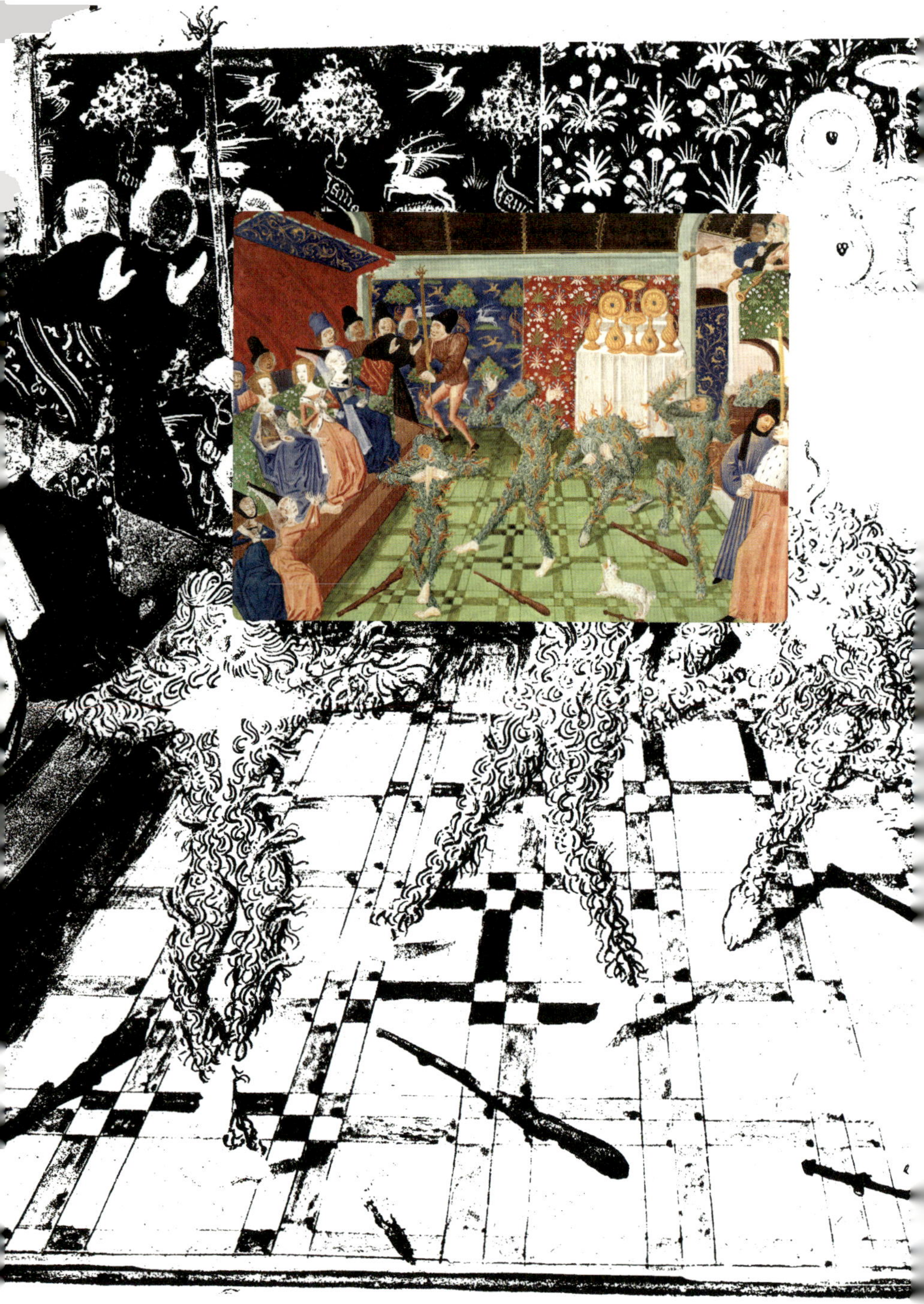

King Charles VI, also known as the Beloved (le Bien-Aimé) and the Mad (French: le Fol or le Fou), was the King of France from 1380 to 1422. He suffered from bouts of insanity where he believed he was made of glass. On January 28, 1393, he was badly burned and four others died from a fire that engulfed the wedding party and became known as the Bal des Ardents.

I wish I could say I was purified by the fire, but all it did was hurt. One man jumped into the wine barrel and was saved, some were pissed on by people who watched from the balconies above, some were thrown into the Seine,

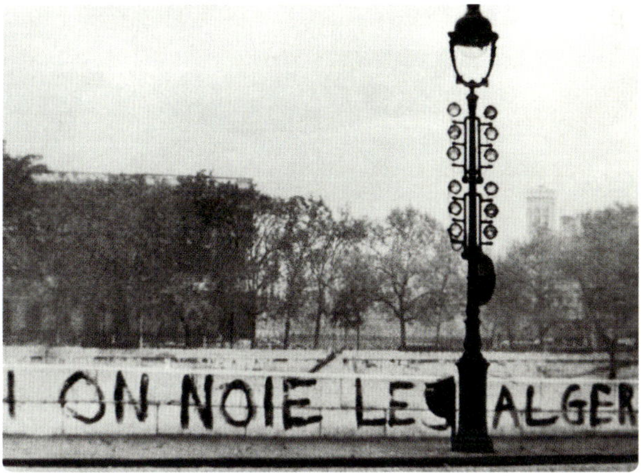

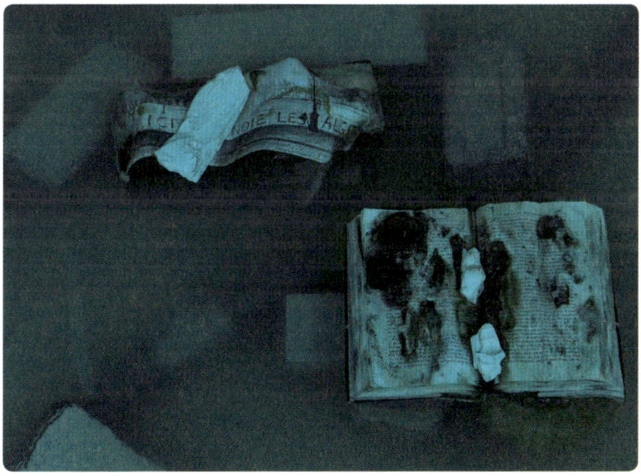

and I, I went inside a dress.

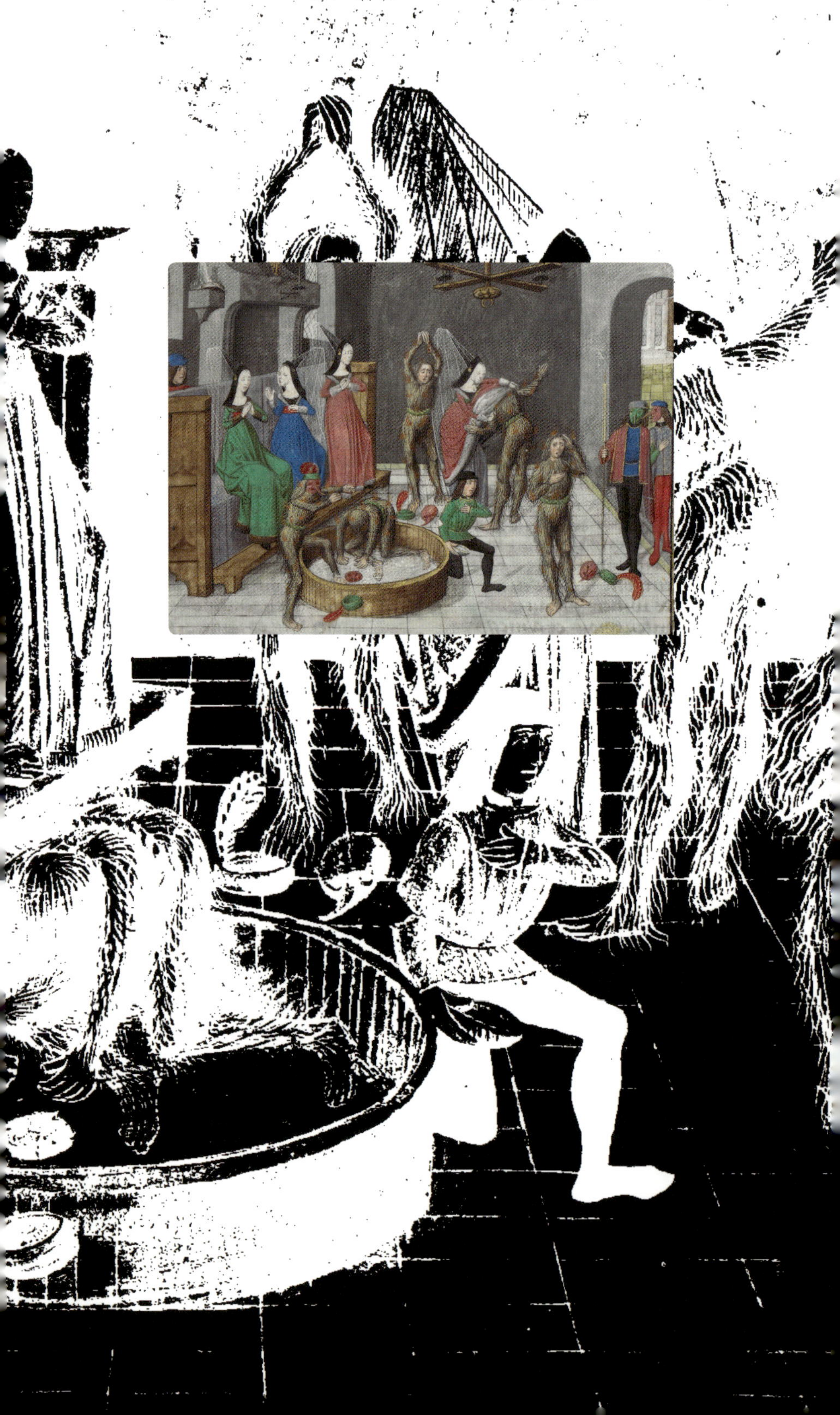

These slides were taken in 1903, a year after the eruption of Mt. Pelée destroyed the city of St. Pierre. St. Pierre was the biggest city in Martinique at the time and was nicknamed the "Paris of the Antilles" for its bustling cosmopolitan atmosphere as well as its liberal sexual mores: a city of excess. It took just a few seconds for the city to be destroyed in its entirety, there were only a handful of survivors. This inspired a new name, "Our Sodom."

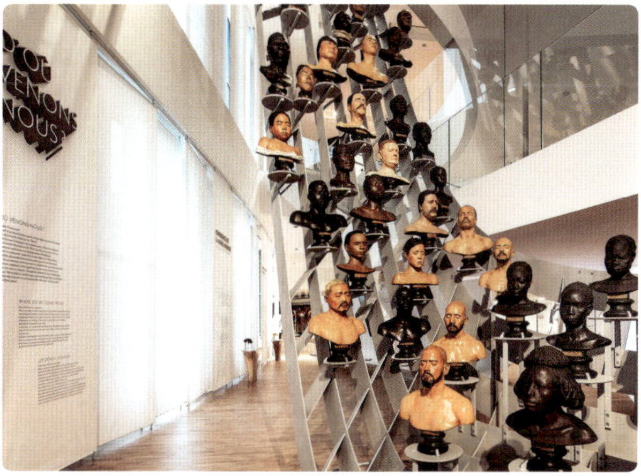

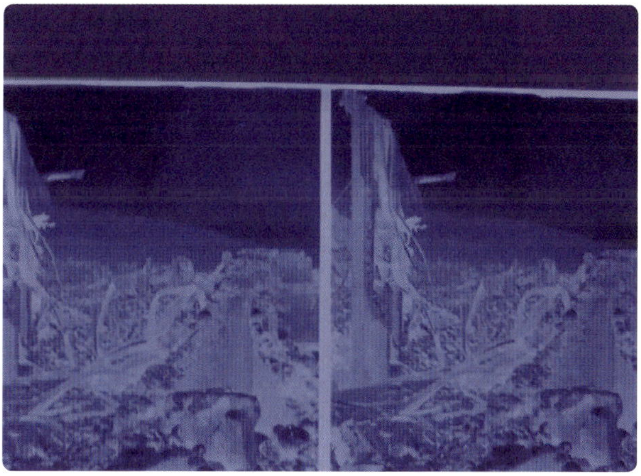

At the time I found these glass slides in the archives at the Smithsonian, I was reading C.L.R. James's classic history of the Haitian Revolution, **The Black Jacobins**, and I saw the images of rubble—burned, exploded buildings and razed landscapes—as a strange surrogate to the images of uprising in my mind, displaced by 1,300 kilometers and 100 years. As I held the glass slides carefully in my white gloves, I felt their granular beginning as sand, black sand from the beaches of the Caribbean. I felt the weight of the material, its polish and promise to be ground into a lens, to be "seen through," to be "on fire."

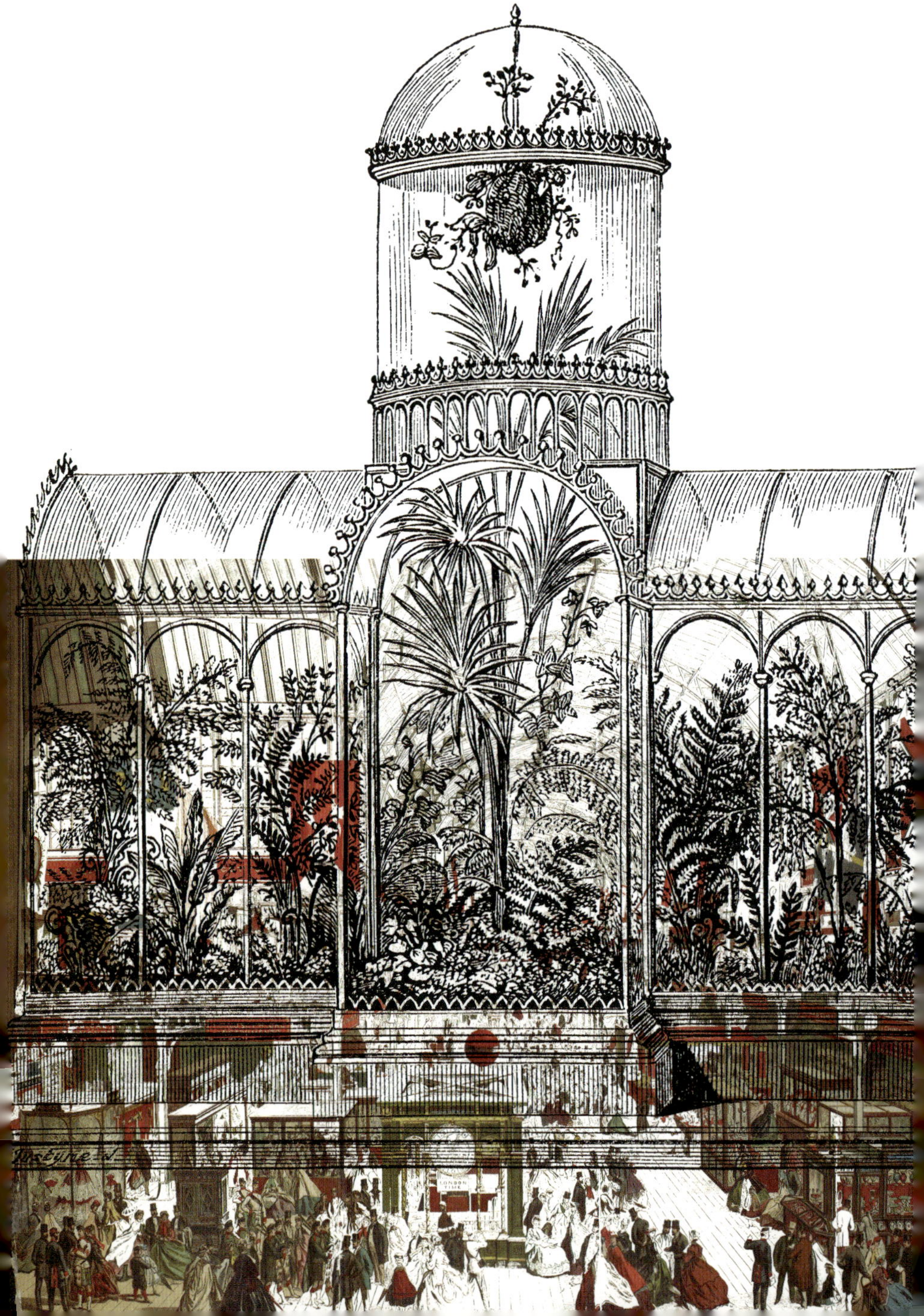

Sometimes my countrymen would carry pieces of glass and mirror with them on their pilgrimages. After a long journey, across a steep, rocky trail to the remote hermitage where the saint's relics were stored, they would take out this small precious piece of glass and hold it in front of the fragment of knucklebone.

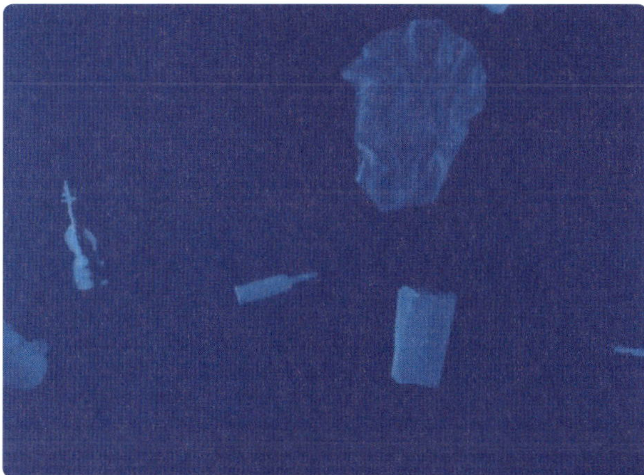

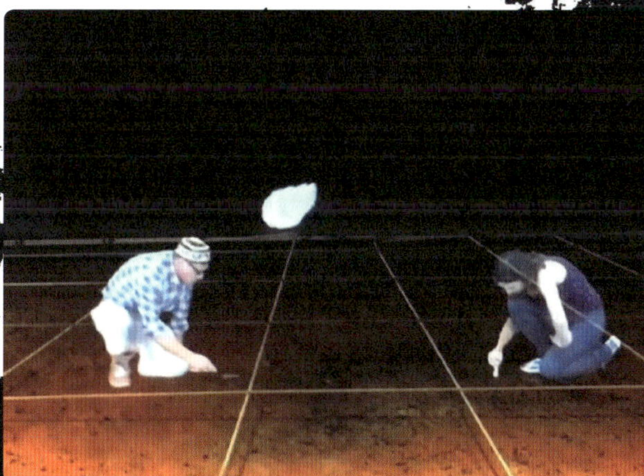

Milieux de culture liquides préparés **au laboratoire de Pasteur. La plupart des ballons qui contiennent ces milieux ont été étiquetés par le Dr Roux.**

The glass operated much like the contemporary iPhone in that it acted acquisitionally. It absorbed the aura of the relic. Though the glass looked no different, no plumper or cloudier, it held the memory of having "seen" the relic.

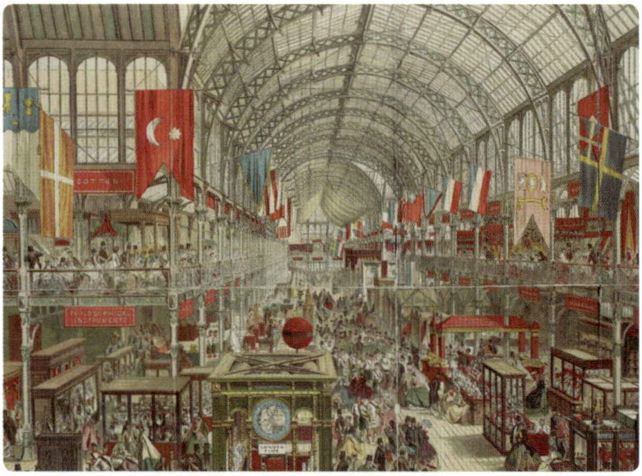

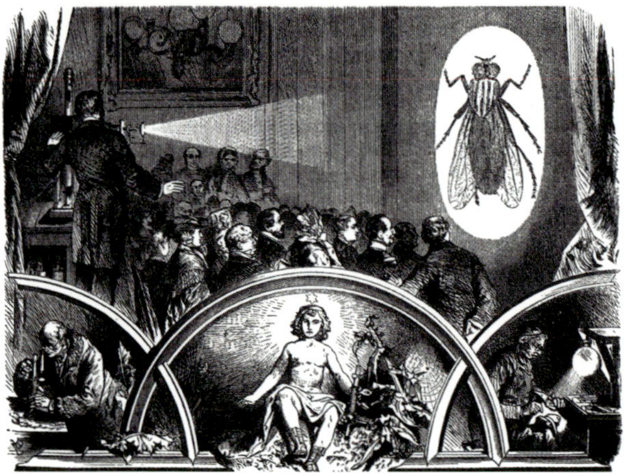

Top: The Great Exhibition in the Crystal Palace, Hyde Park, London, 1851
Bottom: Illustration of a magical lantern lecture (using glass slides) projecting images of early microscopy

When you played the glass back, you could recover a perfect replica of the object that came before. In this way, books were made and history became a thing, much as you know it today. You could say, "This is crystal clear." You could say, "it's in the books." And the argument would be made.

My sovereign body was like an iPhone, a giant refractive lens that took all the Rays of the World into its core, absorbing all the energy without a visible sign of accumulation. Many of the people gathered together and burned their books, they stood outside the buildings of government officials and printing presses, declaring, "we want transparency." One day they gathered outside my window with rocks and banners full of angry slogans. "I see through you," they shouted, as if my future duplicity could be undone. But how could you blame me? I was made of glass.

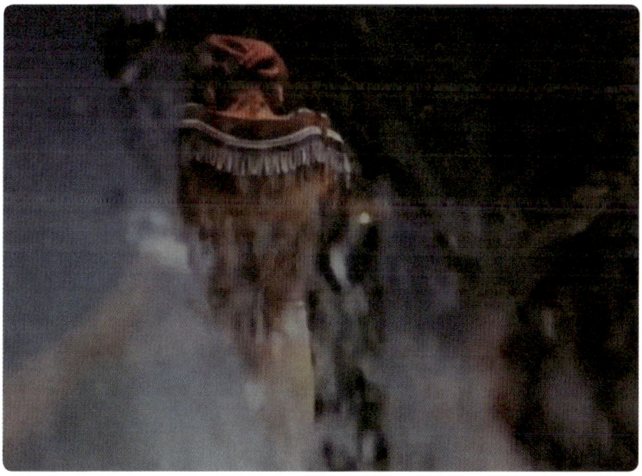

In the next era, glass became common and it was porcelain that was prized.

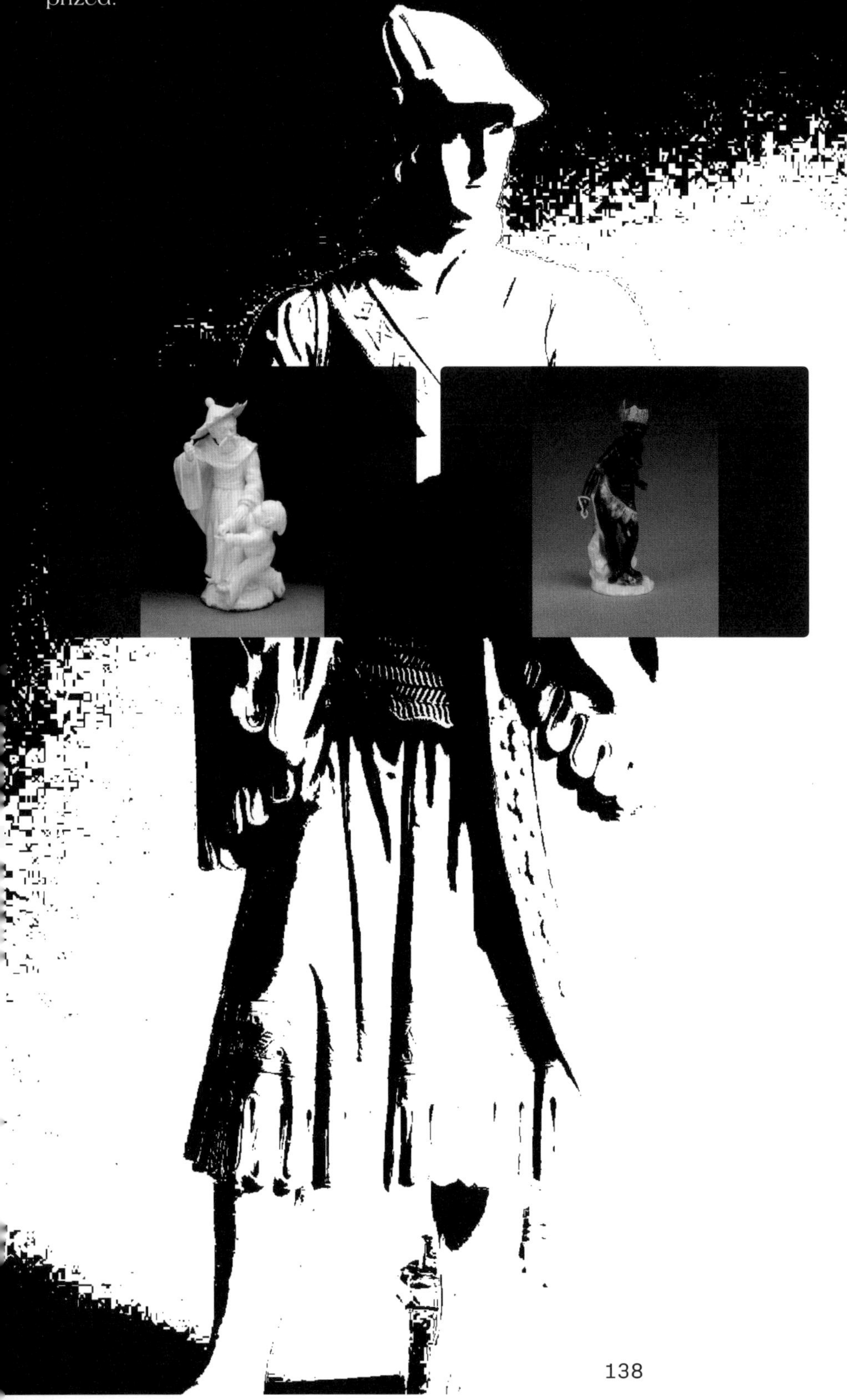

When you held it up to the light it was neither opaque nor transparent, but glowed with pure milky promise. It was delicate but strong. It had the hardness of a superior white body.

The white body comes from outside. It is from America, Italy or China. It is made of kaolin and feldspar. It was genetically engineered on the island of Patmos, it was made from the bones of people who died in the plague. It is impregnable. Nothing can stain it. Not coffee or tea or any other foreign product. Yet because of its small pore size, porcelain was used as a filter, protecting armies against cholera and other bacterial diseases.

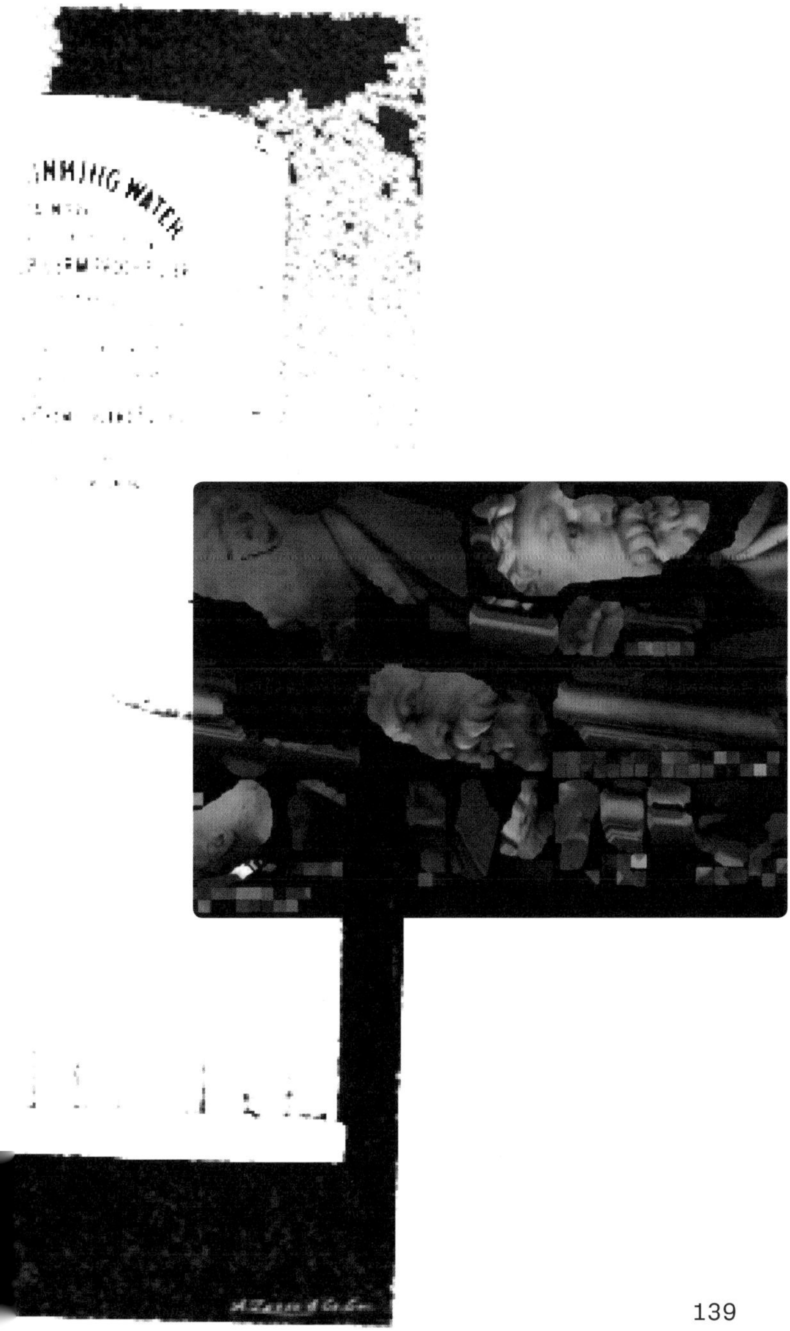

Similarly, survivalists suggest the use of clean white socks or white sheets packed into a cylinder with the water poured through them as an emergency filtration device.

On board the ship the **Étoile**, a sheet of sailcloth was affixed in the wake to allow the sailors to dunk each other without risking death by drowning or being eaten by sharks.

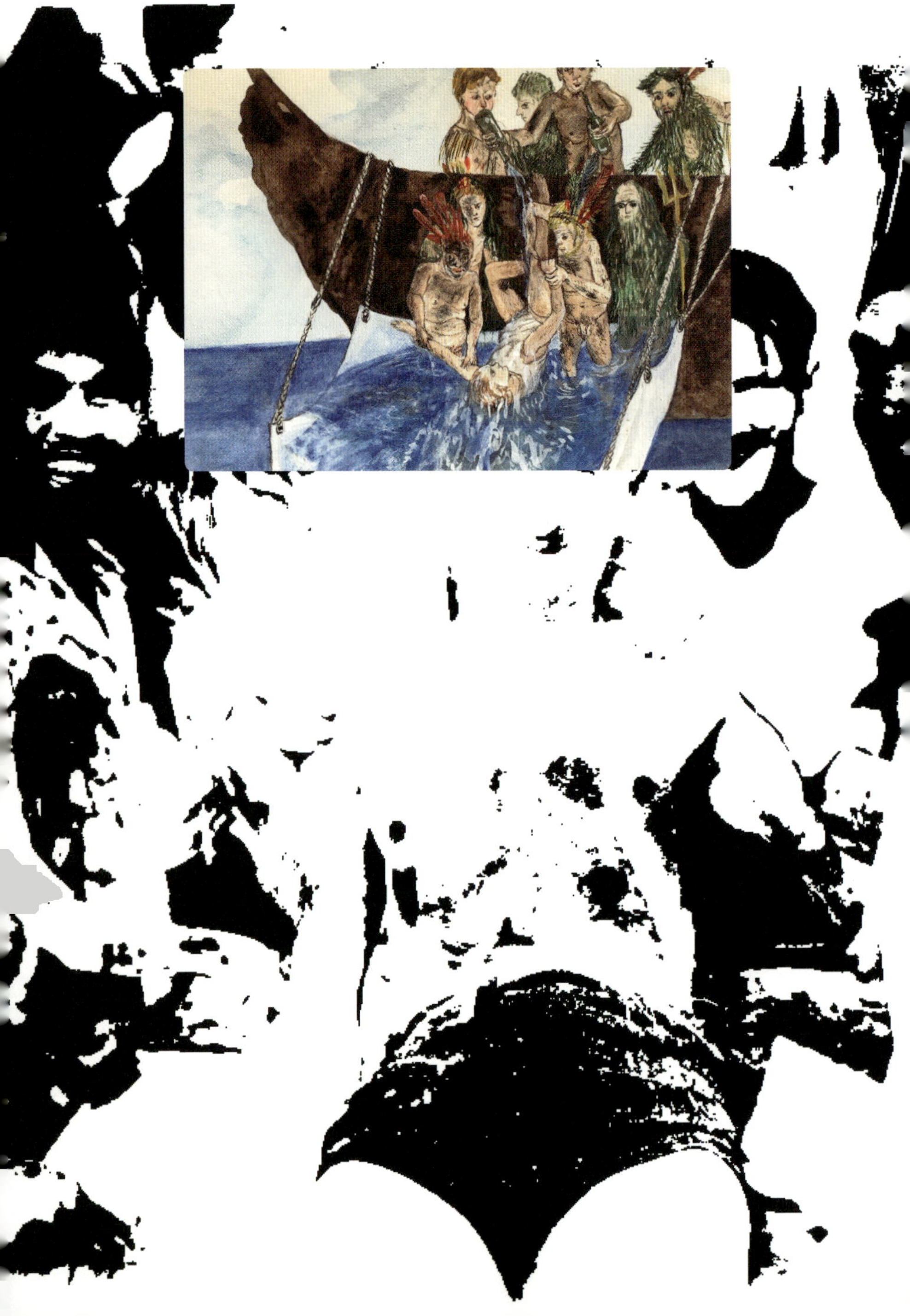

As the ship passed the equator, Jeanne Baret and the other new sailors were dunked by more experienced sailors dressed as "devils." The costume of a devil involved being darkened with soot and tar and decorated with feathers. As Jeanne awaited her dunking, she was the only one who was not naked or stripped to the waist. When the crew began to whisper rumors that perhaps this botanist's assistant was not the man he claimed to be, Jeanne concocted a story that explained she was a eunuch, and the sailors empathized with the implication that she had been a captive of the Ottoman Turks, who perhaps kept her as a slave in a harem. In the privacy of the small cabin below deck, Jeanne fastened the torn strips of linen sheeting closer to her chest, where the irritated skin was blistering into a chronic rash.

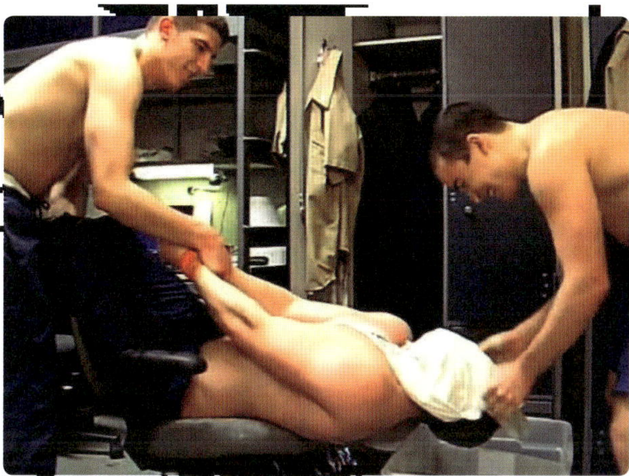

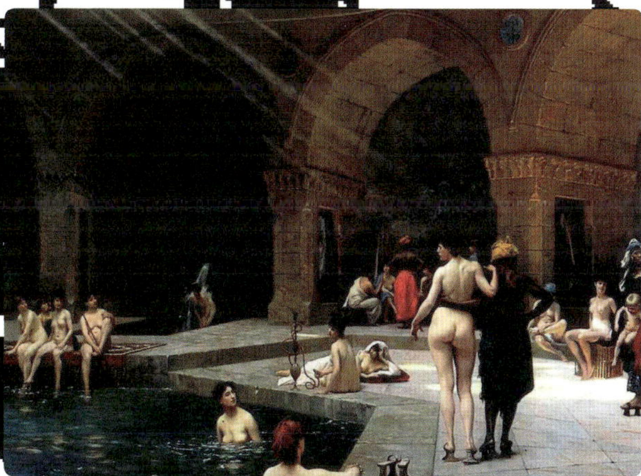

When I was a king, the Beloved, the one they wrapped in sheets and blankets to keep from breaking, you took this photo in Istanbul.
When James Baldwin was in Istanbul, he heard of a magician who could hypnotize crowds.

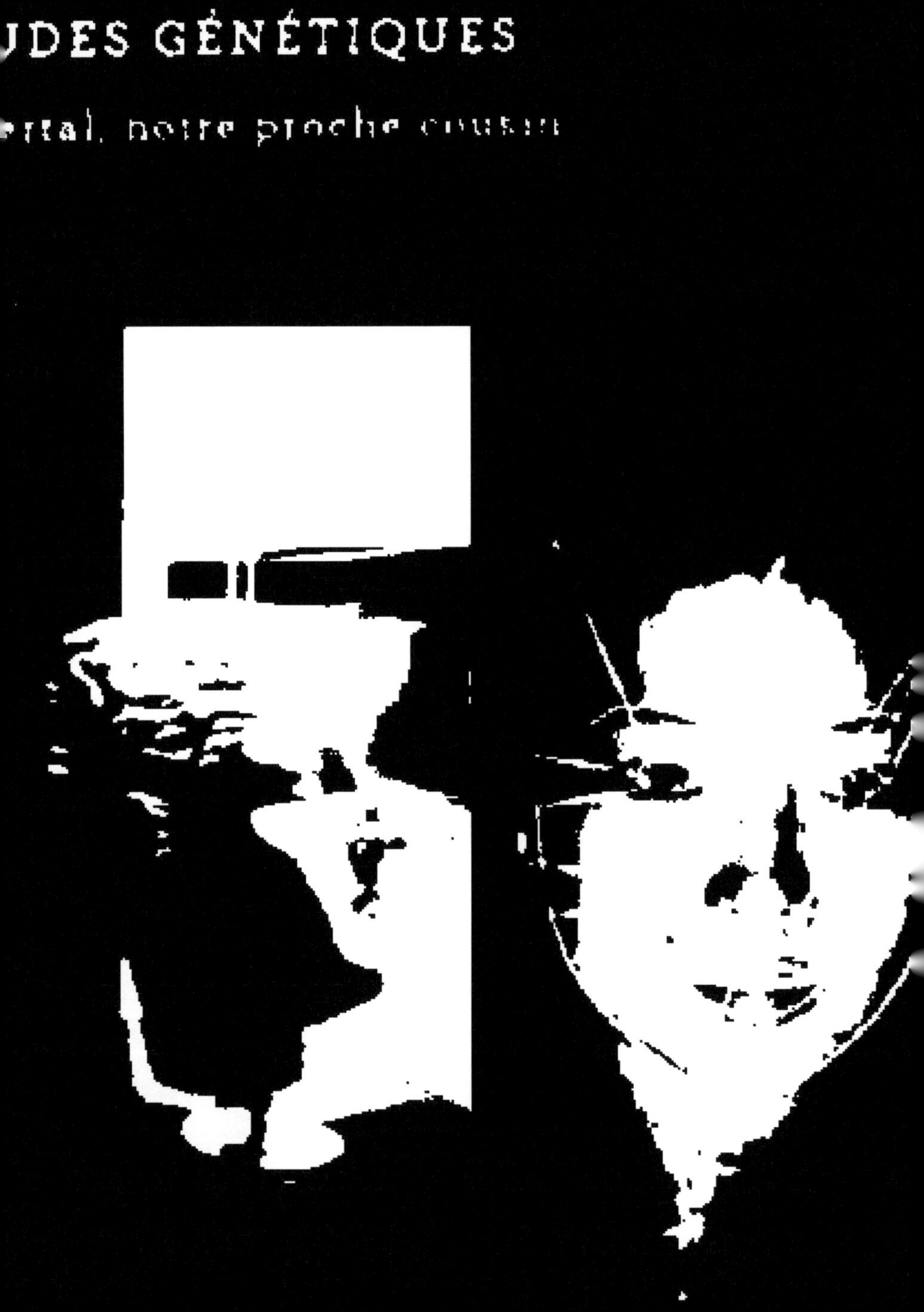

At first, Baldwin's friends laughed at the magician's stage name, "Morgan," assuming this was a mistake of language or culture based on a conflation of Merlin and Morgan le Fay. Baldwin said, "perhaps he she knows exactly what their name means; let's invite this magician to visit us."

HING NEANDERTAL

RE d'une RENCONTRE

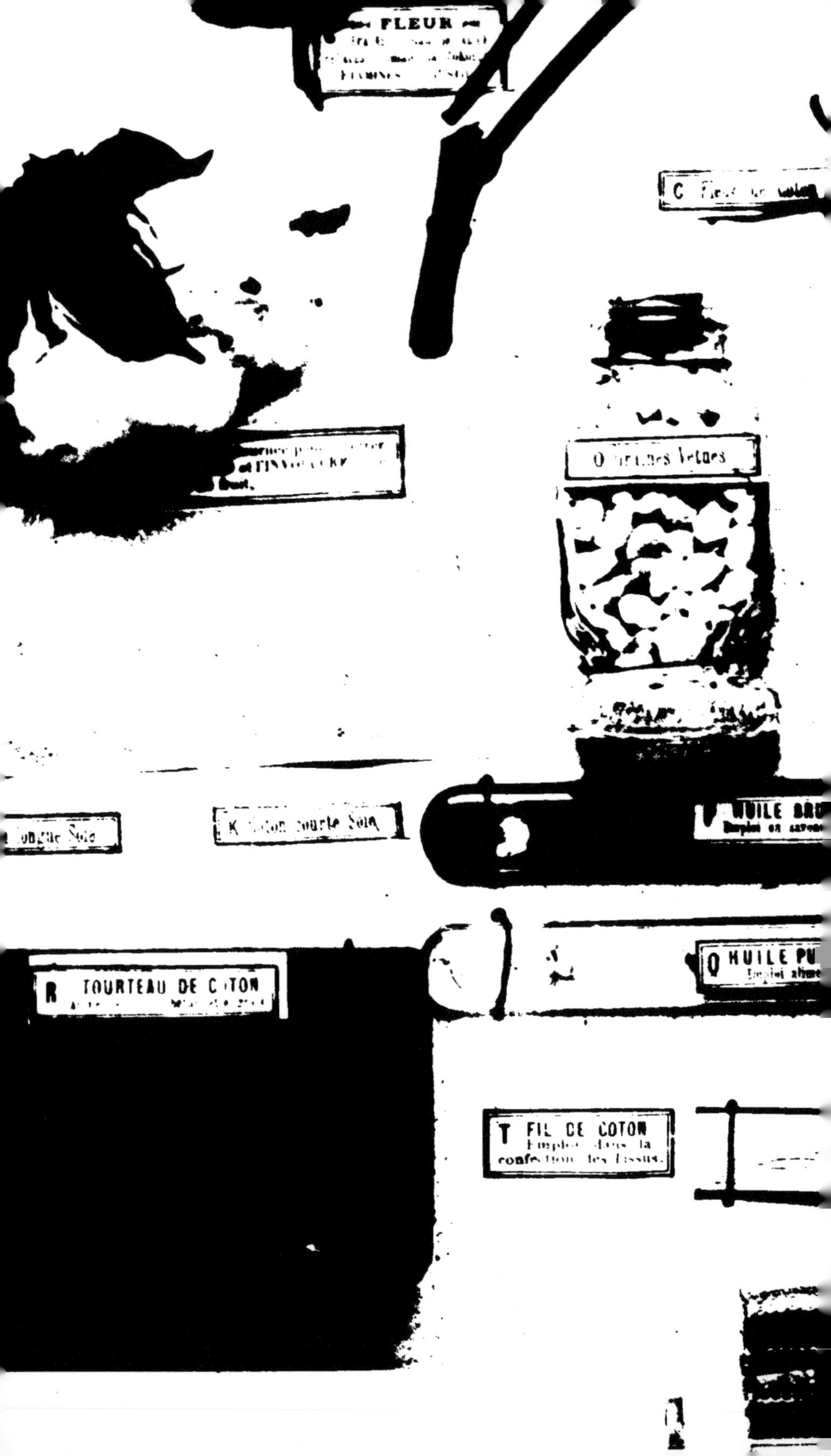
FLEUR
K coton courte Soie
R TOURTEAU DE COTON
T FIL DE COTON
Emploi dans la
confection des tissus.

The magician had an ominous negative aura. Morgan was known for taking advantage of people under trances, making their bodies gyrate with sexual improprieties that shamed them for life when they woke up from their trances and heard what it was they had done.

As Baldwin and his friend sat across from Morgan, Morgan suggested to the friend that he was very tired, and after the friend had fallen asleep at this suggestion, Morgan told Baldwin to wait naked in the bed. He thought he was waiting for Morgan to disrobe in the bathroom, but suddenly, somehow, Morgan and the magician's assistant, a young man, came into the room and began to beat him violently, kicking and punching his face and body.

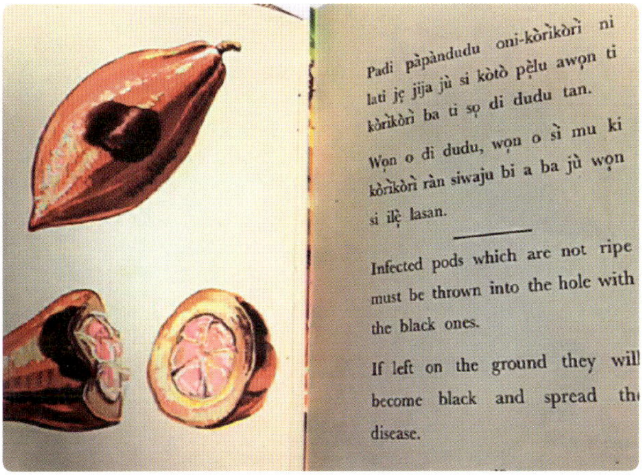

Photo of an educational booklet made to instruct local farmers in French colonies how to properly grow and cultivate colonial products

Black Panther Party leader Eldridge Cleaver wrote that James Baldwin was "a white man inside a black body." According to Cleaver, Baldwin's homosexuality (and the way it infused his writing) expressed a "sycophantic" relationship to whites, hatred for his own black people, and a "racial death-wish."

I think of porcelain and the filters made of this material that separated the tiny bodies of bacteria from the liquid they lived within. And it was through porcelain and these bacterial studies that we learned of viruses, a class of beings small enough to pass through the white body, to make it "go mulatto," or so the phrase went when describing the symptoms of the tobacco plant sickness, TMV, in terms of racial "degradation": the wooly texture, the yellowing leaves. So small that the finest material could not catch it, the virus went on, neither dead nor alive, though its shadowy existence wrote question marks around the very notion of what it meant to be truly alive.

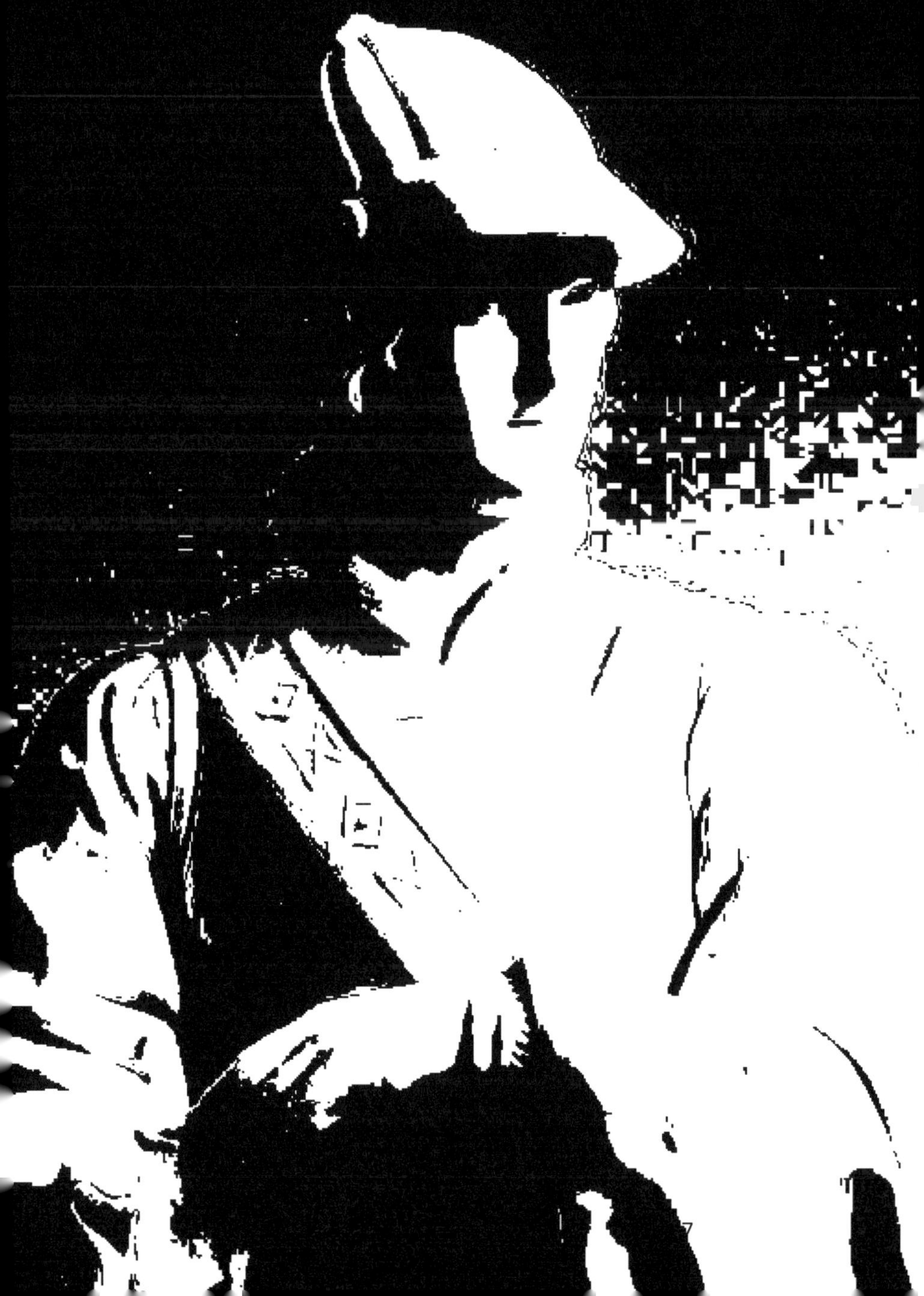

When I was the Beloved one, the one they swaddled in heavy duvets and linen sheets,

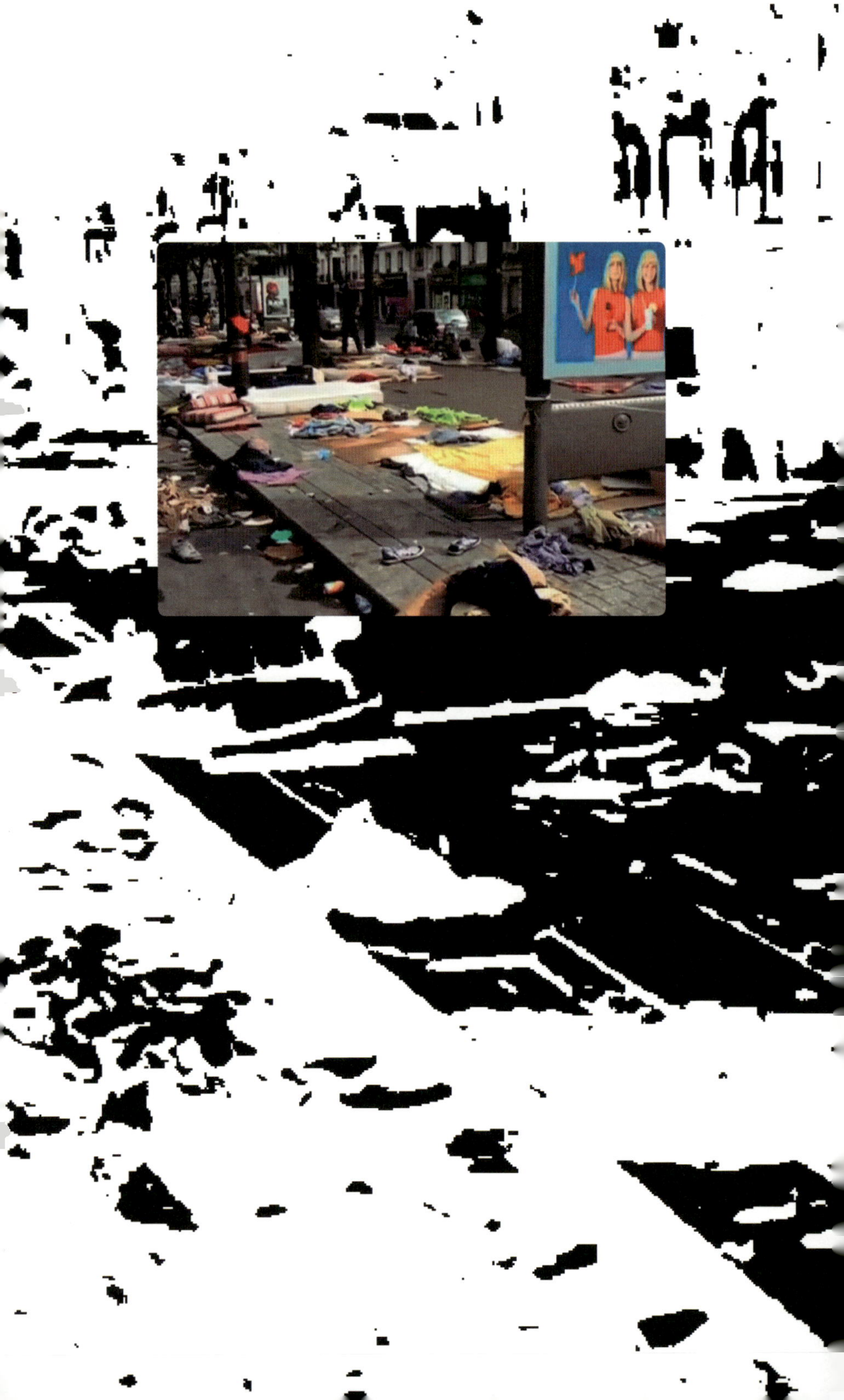

you took this photo in Istanbul, while I kept my face averted from you, afraid of the grief and terror that might break open and spill across the room if you were to see the markings he had made.

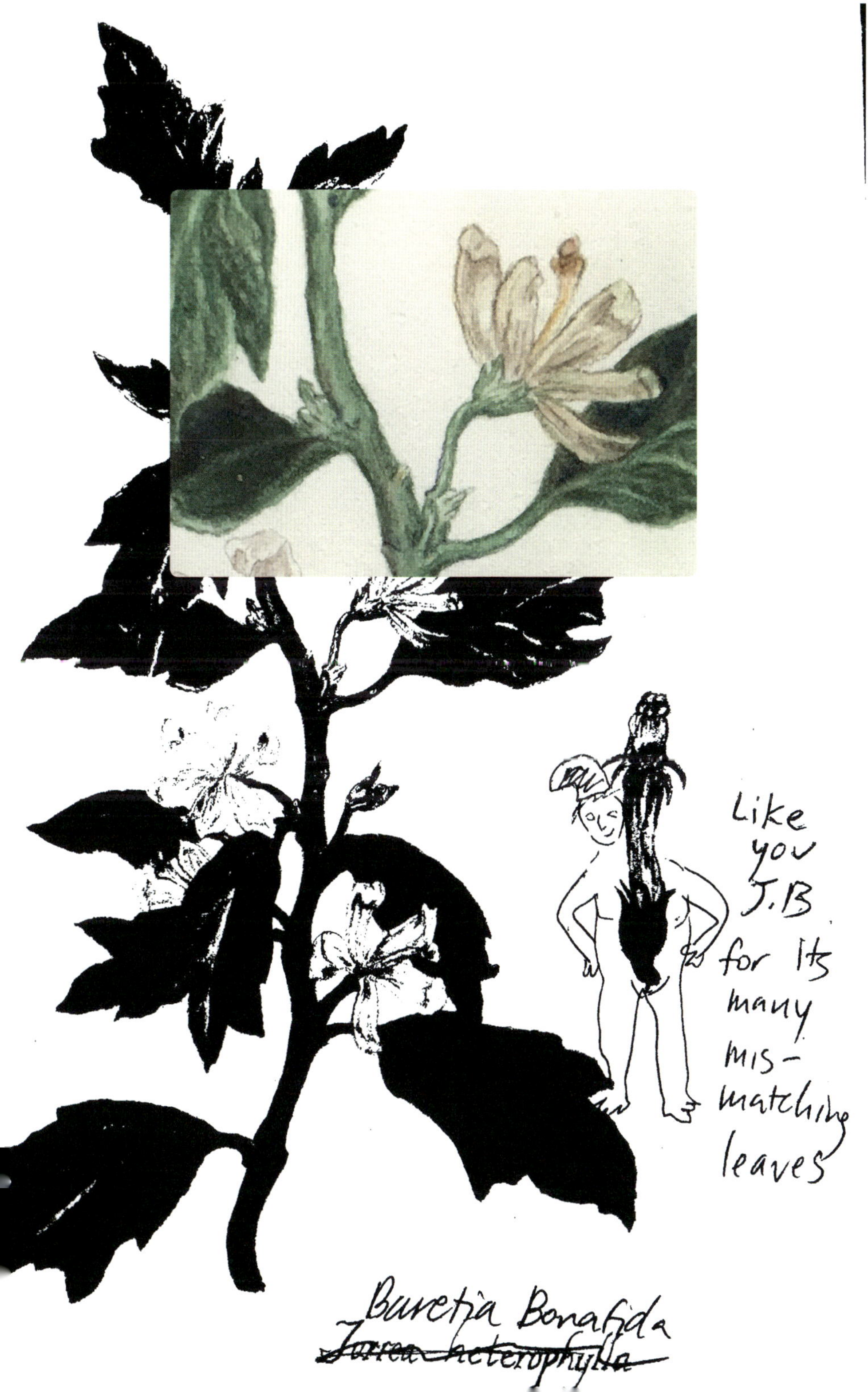

I think of you here, turned away from me, away from the future that waits in vain for the past to roll over and offer itself up.

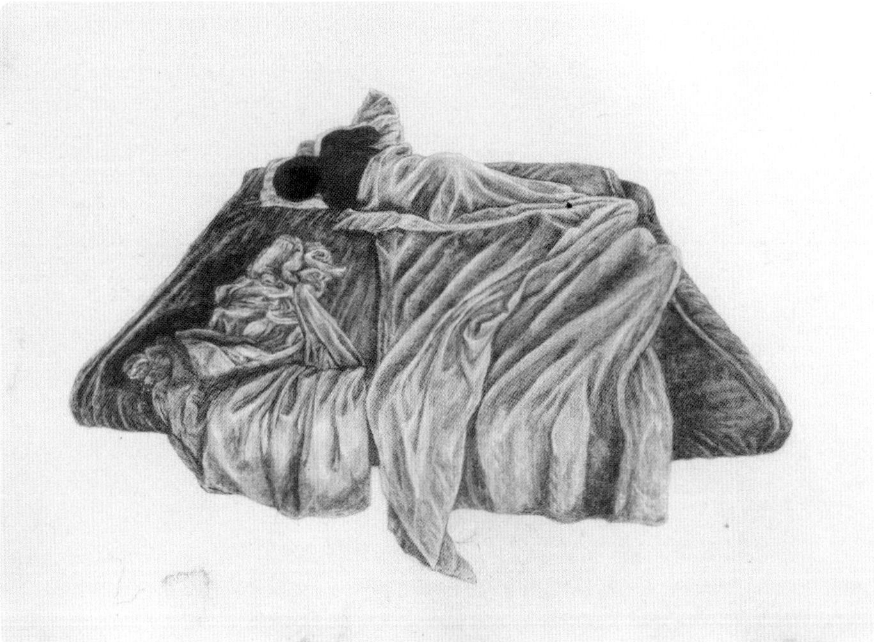

WORKS IN THE EXHIBITION

Unless otherwise noted, all works are by Candice Lin and are courtesy of the artist and François Ghebaly, Los Angeles, and were presented at all three venues:

(BCAR)
Bétonsalon – Center for Art and Research, Paris

(P)
Portikus, Frankfurt am Main

(RDLCA)
Reva and David Logan Center for the Arts at the University of Chicago

This listing reflects the most complete information available at the time of publication. Credits for source materials, related acknowledgments, and additional information about the components of selected works appear on page 159.

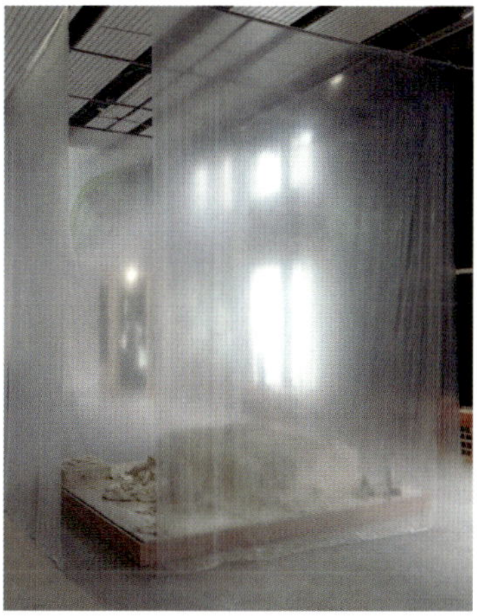

A Hard White Body. 2017
Porcelain, wood, plastic sheeting, urinal, pipes, distillation system, bricks, buckets, water from the Seine river, urine, plants, and misting system
(BCAR)

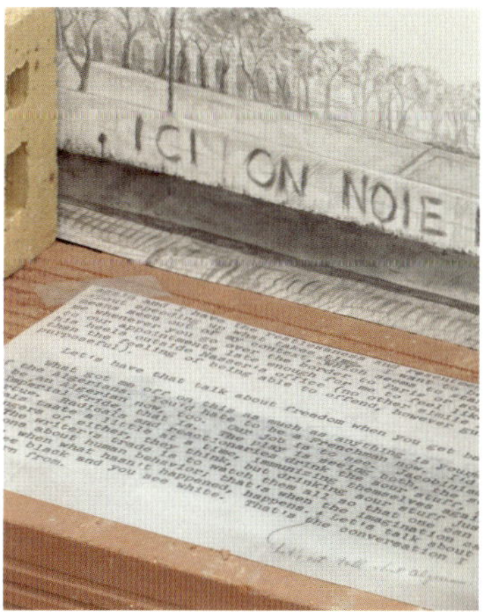

The Wake, Under Construction 2017
Bricks, porcelain, wood, cardboard, books, photographs, paper, plants, and alcohol
(BCAR)

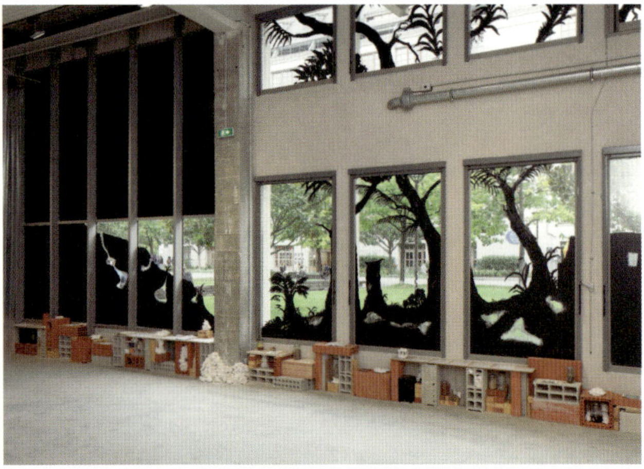

“We demand the right to opacity” . . . 2017
Paint, soap, and calcium carbonate
(BCAR)

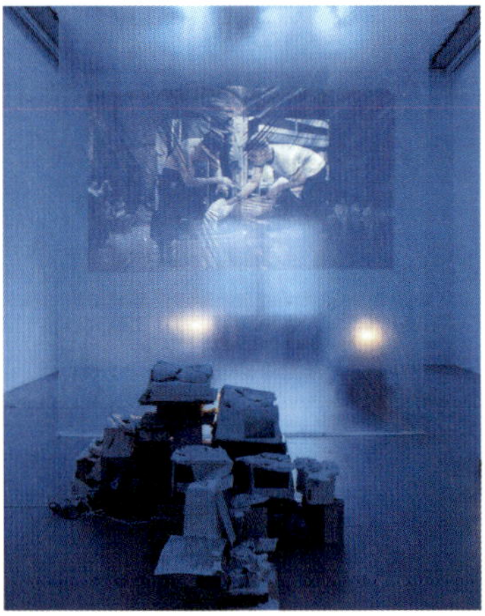

A Hard White Body 2017–18
Porcelain, bricks, wood, pipes, plants, cardboard, books, photographs, paper, used clothing, dried plants, glass jars, hot plate, kettle, pitcher, silkworms, heating wire, distillation system, and urine
(P)

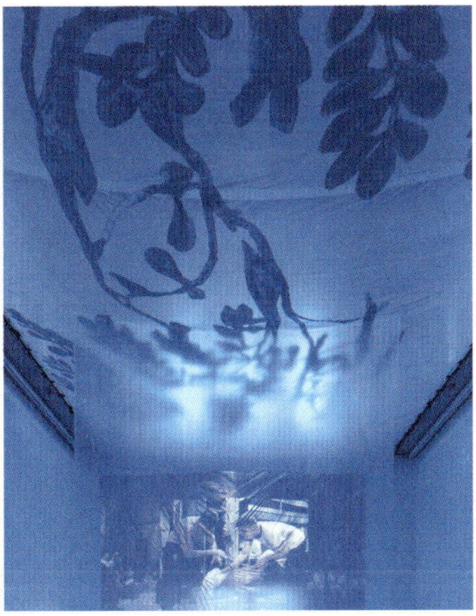

Under the Shadow of the Peacock Flower
. . . . 2018
Paint and plastic sheeting
(P)

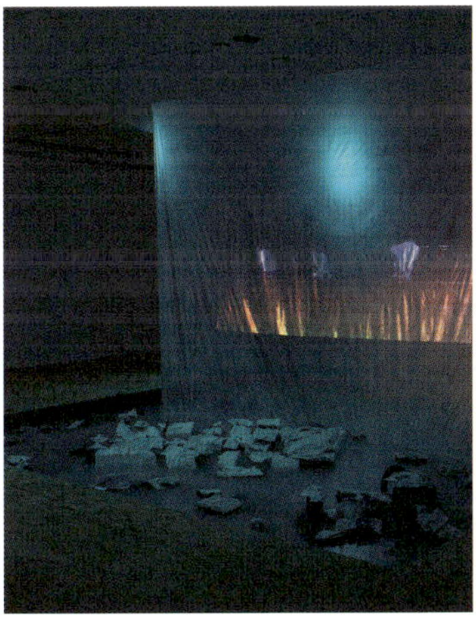

A Hard White Body 2018
Porcelain, bricks, wood, pipes, pumps, plastic sheeting, books, photographs, drawings, printed material, dried and live plants, glass jars, distillation system, and urine
(RDLCA)

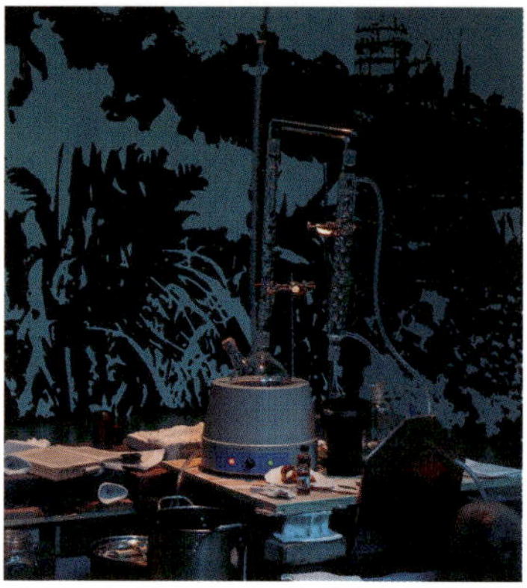

Refined by Fire 2018
Burned pedestal, pit-fired ceramic skull, vaporizer, custom scent, burnt sugar and bones, hot plate, wall paintings, and bone-black pigment

Commissioned by Logan Center Exhibitions, University of Chicago
(RDLCA)

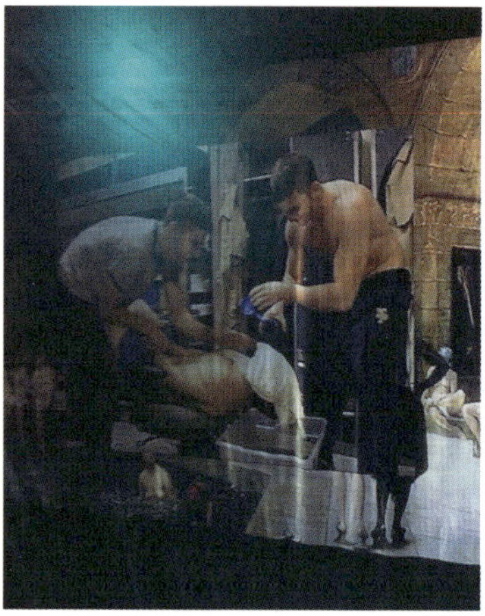

The Beloved 2017
Single-channel video with sound, 12 min.

Voiceover by Victoria Aravindhan
CGI animation and renderings by Chase Stutzman
(BCAR, P, RDLCA)

CONTRIBUTORS

The work of **CANDICE LIN** engages notions of gender, race, and sexuality, drawing from post/de-colonialism, citizen science, anthropology, and feminist and queer theory. Lin has presented solo exhibitions at Portikus, Frankfurt am Main (2018); Bétonsalon – Center for Art and Research & Villa Vassilieff, Paris (2017); Gasworks, London (2016); and Commonwealth & Council, Los Angeles (2016). She has also exhibited widely in recent group exhibitions at Moderna Museet, Stockholm; New Museum, New York; HANGAR, Lisbon; Sculpture Center, New York; and Galeria Fortes Vilaça, São Paulo. A recipient of the Louis Comfort Tiffany Foundation Award (2017), Lin recently completed residencies at Centre les Récollets, Paris (2017), and Headlands Center for the Arts, Sausalito, California (2016). Lin received her MFA in the New Genres program at the San Francisco Art Institute in 2004 and her BA in Visual Art and Art Semiotics at Brown University, Providence, Rhode Island, in 2001.

Writer and curator **LOTTE ARNDT** engages with the work of artists who critically interrogate the postcolonial present and the blind spots of modernity. She co-curated **A Hard White Body** (2017) at Bétonsalon – Center for Art and Research & Villa Vassilieff, Paris, and **A Hard White Body, a Soft White Worm** (2018) at Portikus, Frankfurt am Main. Recent projects include **Tampered Emotions: Lust for Dust**, Triangle France, Marseille (2018); **One Sentence Exhibition**, Kadist (online; 2018); and the research program **The Vacation of the Museum: Decolonize Ethnographic Collections with Cinema** (2016–18). She was a 2016 Goethe-Institut fellow at Villa Vassilieff, Paris, and subsequently served as guest editor of the online magazine **Qalqalah** (2017). She works closely with the French artists and writers' group Ruser l'image and is a member of the research group Global Art Prospective. She publishes on artistic strategies that aim to subvert Eurocentric narratives and institutions and co-organizes cultural programs, screenings, and discussions in artistic and academic spaces.

YESOMI UMOLU is Artistic Director of the 2019 Chicago Architecture Biennial and Director and Curator at Logan Center Exhibitions at the University of Chicago, where she also lectures on art history and visual culture. Specializing in global contemporary art and spatial practices, Umolu recently curated **Cinthia Marcelle and Tiago Mata Machado: Divine Violence** (2017), **Kapwani Kiwanga: The sum and its parts** (2017), and **So-called Utopias** (2015). Prior to joining the Logan Center, Umolu held curatorial positions at the Eli and Edythe Broad Art Museum at Michigan State University, East Lansing; the Walker Art Center, Minneapolis; and Manifesta 8, Murcia, Spain. Umolu holds an MA in Architectural Design from the University of Edinburgh and an MA in Curating Contemporary Art from the Royal College of Art, London. She is a 2016 recipient of a curatorial research fellowship from the Andy Warhol Foundation for the Visual Arts.

RIZVANA BRADLEY is an assistant professor of Film and Media Studies and African-American Studies at Yale University, New Haven, Connecticut. She holds a BA from Williams College, Williamstown, Massachusetts, and a PhD from Duke University, Durham, North Carolina. A former Helena Rubinstein Curatorial Fellow at the Whitney Museum of American Art, New York, Bradley focuses her research and teaching on the study of film and media at the intersections of literature, poetry, contemporary art, and performance. Her approach to artistic production within African-American culture and the wider black diaspora expands and develops frameworks for thinking across global and transnational artistic and cinematic practices. Bradley is currently at work on two new scholarly book projects and has published articles in **Women and Performance: A Journal of Feminist Theory**, **TDR: The Drama Review**, **Discourse: Journal for Theoretical Studies in Media and Culture**, **Rhizomes: Cultural Studies in Emerging Knowledge**, and **Black Camera: An International Film Journal**.

MEL Y. CHEN is an associate professor of Gender and Women's Studies and Director of the Center for the Study of Sexual Culture at the University of California, Berkeley. Their first book, **Animacies: Biopolitics, Racial Mattering, and Queer Affect** (Duke University Press, 2012; MLA Alan Bray Award), explores questions of racialization, queering, gender, disability, and affective economies in animate and inanimate "life" through the extended concept of animacy. Their current book project concerns relationships among the conceptual territories of toxicity and intoxication and related histories of the shared interanimation of race and disability with particular attention to gender and materiality. Elsewhere, they write on slowness, gesture, inhumanisms, and cognitive disability and method. They co-edit a book series entitled **Anima** with Jasbir

K. Puar at Duke University Press and are part of a small and sustaining queer of color arts collective in the San Francisco Bay Area.

JIH-FEI CHENG is an assistant professor in the Department of Feminist, Gender, and Sexuality Studies at Scripps College, Claremont, California. He has worked in HIV/AIDS social services, managed a cultural center, been involved in media production and curating, and participated in grassroots organizations serving queer communities of color in Los Angeles and New York. Cheng's research examines the intersections of science, media, surveillance, and social movements. His first book manuscript explores the ways the experimental videos produced by feminist and queer of color AIDS activists during the early crisis years (1980s to early 1990s) in the US continue to intervene in contemporary popular media, scientific conceptions, and politics, tracking a long history of virology and media representation that began with the late nineteenth-century discovery of the first virus in a tobacco plant. His writings have appeared in **Amerasia Journal**, **Catalyst: Feminism, Theory, Technoscience**, and **Women's Studies Quarterly**, among other publications.

C. RILEY SNORTON is a cultural theorist whose work focuses on race, gender, and sexuality. He is a professor of English and Gender and Sexuality Studies at the University of Chicago and the author of **Nobody is Supposed to Know: Black Sexuality on the Down Low** (University of Minnesota Press, 2014) and **Black on Both Sides: A Racial History of Trans Identity** (University of Minnesota Press, 2017), which received a Stonewall Book Award and a Lambda Literary Award for Transgender Nonfiction in 2018. Snorton's research has been supported by the Ford Foundation, the Andrew W. Mellon Foundation, and the National Endowment for the Humanities, and his writings have appeared in **SOULS: A Critical Journal of Black Politics, Culture and Society**, **The Black Scholar**, **GLQ: A Journal of Gay and Lesbian Studies**, and **TSQ: Transgender Studies Quarterly**.

Photography Credits

Unless otherwise noted, all works by Candice Lin are © the artist and are reproduced by permission of the artist. Additional image credits appear on page 160.

Figures in illustrations:

Arndt, Elective Affinities: Fig. 2: Mathilde Assier. Fig. 3: Claudia Famulok. Lin and Snorton, In Dialogue: Fig. 1: Robert Chase Heishman. Fig. 4: Helena Schlichting. Chen and Cheng, A (Post-) Apocolyptic Call to Knowledge and Action: Fig. 1: Ian Byers Gamber. Fig. 2: Tim Bowditch. Bradley, Minor Ecologies: Figs. 1, 3, 4: Jeff McLane. Figs. 5, 7: Andy Keate. Fig. 8: Chen Yung-Jen.

Visual essay by Candice Lin:

Every reasonable attempt has been made to identify owners of copyright. Errors or omissions will be corrected in any subsequent editions.

Unless otherwise noted, images are stills from Candice Lin, *The Beloved*, 2017. Courtesy the artist and François Ghebaly, Los Angeles

"Precipitous Descent of a Cordillera of the Andes in the Province of Choco," from *Journal of a residence and travels in Colombia during the years 1823 and 1824*, Vol. 2, 1825. John Carter Brown Library at Brown University

Philibert Commerson, Bougainvillea spectabilis, 1767–68. Department of Collections, Herbier national, Spécimen P00169376. Image © Muséum national d'Histoire naturelle, Paris

"Jeanne Baret," from *Navigazioni di Cook pel grande oceano e intorno al globo*. Vol. 2, 1916. State Library of New South Wales, M 980/CO1/22A1-22A7, FL3740703

Table des plantes médicamenteuses, 18th century. Archives of Philibert Commerson, Department of Collections, Central Library, Ms 884, Image © Muséum national d'Histoire naturelle, Paris

Georg Dionysius Ehret, *The Basis of Carl Linnaeus's Sexual System for the Classification of Flowering Plants*, 1736. Natural History Museum, London

Rouarge Brothers, *Bougainville drops anchor in Tahiti*, from *Les Navigateurs français: histoire des navigations, découvertes et colonisations françaises*, 1846

Louis-Antoine de Bougainville's expedition to Tahiti, 1768. Bibliothèque nationale de France

Research image of the Pasteur Museum, Paris, as fragmented by a 3D scanning phone application. Original photo: Lucas Morin

Detail of "Dance of the Wodewoses" from Jean Froissart, *Chroniques*, Vol. IV, part 2, 15th century. The British Library. Image © The British Library Board, MS Harley 4380 f001r

Jean Texier, photograph of the Saint-Michel Bridge, from *L'Humanité*, October 17, 1961

Untitled image from Jean Froissart, *Chroniques*, 15th century. The British Library. Image © The British Library Board, Royal MS 18 E.ii f206r

Installation view of *Qui sommes-nous?*, Musée de l'Homme, National Museum of Natural History, Paris. Photo: Jean-Christophe Domenech

"Wardian case," from *The National Magazine*, 1856. The University Library, University of Illinois at Urbana-Champaign

The Great Exhibition in the Crystal Palace, Hyde Park, London, 1851. The British Library. Image © The British Library Board, Add. MS 35255

Glass at Pasteur Museum, Paris. Photo: Lucas Morin

Illustration of a magical lantern lecture using glass slides

Sèvres Porcelain Factory, *Jean d'Orléans, comte de Dunois et de Longueville*, 1823. Royal Collection Trust / Image © Her Majesty Queen Elizabeth II 2019

Agostino Carlini for Derby Porcelain Factory, *Touch*, 18th century. Victoria & Albert Museum, London, Given by Lady Charlotte Schreiber, 414:140-1885

Johann Friedrich Eberlein for Meissen, *Africa*, 18th century. Victoria & Albert Museum, London, Bequeathed by Miss Florence Augusta Beare in memory of Arthur Doveton Clarke, C.943-1919

Pasteur-Chamberland filter at the Pasteur Museum, Paris. Photo: Lucas Morin

Research image of a bust of Charles Chamberland at the Pasteur Museum, Paris, fragmented by a 3D scanning phone application. Original photo: Lucas Morin

Photograph of the naval ritual of "Crossing the Line," ca. 1942–45. Joseph George Freiberger Collection (AFC/2001/001/94626), Veterans History Project, American Folklife Center, Library of Congress, Washington, D.C.

Candice Lin, *Reimagining of the naval ritual "Crossing of the Line," based on engravings and photographs depicting the evolution of this equatorial ritual from the 18th century onward*, 2017

Jean-Léon Gérôme, *The Grand Bath at Bursa*, 1885. Private collection.

Still from a YouTube video of three young men demonstrating waterboarding, October 28, 2009, https://www.youtube.com/watch?v=DiXs3zhe1vE

Cotton school box prepared before the war by M. Prudhomme. Colonial Garden - Ministry of the Colonies, Paris. Image © CIRAD

Candice Lin, *The plant you would have been (Jeanne Baret)*, 2017. Photo: Kell Yang-Sammataro

Candice Lin, *James Baldwin sleeping in Istanbul (after a photo by Sedat Pakay)*, 2017. Photo: Kell Yang-Sammataro

This publication was produced in conjunction with the exhibitions *A Hard White Body/Un corps blanc exquis* (September 6–December 23, 2017), curated by Lotte Arndt and Lucas Morin and organized by Bétonsalon–Center for Art and Research & Villa Vassilieff, Paris; *A Hard White Body, a Soft White Worm* (February 10–April 8, 2018), curated by Lotte Arndt, Lucas Morin, and Philippe Pirotte and organized by Portikus, Frankfurt am Main; and *A Hard White Body, a Porous Slip* (September 14–October 28, 2018), curated by Yesomi Umolu and organized by Logan Center Exhibitions at the Reva and David Logan Center for the Arts at the University of Chicago.

BÉTONSALON — CENTRE D'ART ET DE RECHERCHE VILLA VASSILIEFF   PORTIKUS   Reva and David LOGAN CENTER for the Arts

This book is published by the Reva and David Logan Center for the Arts at the University of Chicago.

Library of Congress Control Number: 2019901952
ISBN: 978-0-692-13836-6

Distributed by The University of Chicago Press

The University of Chicago Press
11030 S. Langley Avenue
Chicago, IL 60628 USA
www.press.uchicago.edu

Support for *Candice Lin: A Hard White Body/Un corps blanc exquis* was provided by the City of Paris, the French Ministry of Culture and Communication, the Île-de-France region, the Daniel and Nina Carasso Foundation, and Perspektive–Fund for Contemporary Art and Architecture.

A Hard White Body, a Soft White Worm received generous financial support from the Hessische Kulturstiftung.

Major support for *A Hard White Body, a Porous Slip* was provided by The Andy Warhol Foundation for the Visual Arts, The Reva and David Logan Foundation, and friends of the Logan Center.

Generous funding for this publication was provided by the Elizabeth Firestone Graham Foundation and Hessische Kulturstiftung. This publication wouldn't have been possible without François Ghebaly, Los Angeles.

Publication Management . . . Alyssa Brubaker and Katja Rivera
Copy Editor and Proofreader . . . Amanda Glesmann

Exhibition Views at Bétonsalon–Center for Art and Research, Paris, photographed by . . . Aurélien Mole (pages 31–32, 34–42, 44–46)
. . . Mathilde Assier (pages 33, 43)

Exhibition Views at Portikus, Frankfurt am Main, photographed by . . . Helena Schlichting (pages 77–81, 83–89).
. . . Claudia Famulok (pages 82, 90)

Exhibition Views at the Reva and David Logan Center for the Arts at the University of Chicago photographed by . . . Robert Chase Heishman (pages 105, 108–118)
. . . Mike Grittani (pages 106, 107)

Design . . . Studio ELLA
Printed by . . . Shapco, Inc.

Cover and Endpapers . . . Candice Lin
A Hard White Body
2017, (detail)